FAR BETTER MONEY MANAGEMENT

Far Better Money MANAGEMENT

NAVIGATING WEALTH WITH PURPOSE AND UNDERSTANDING

JOE CHRISTIAN

FAR BETTER
C O A C H I N G

ISBN: 978-1-7357818-2-2

e-ISBN: 978-1-7357818-3-9

Book cover and layout design:
Joanna & Grzegorz Japoł - LUNA Design Studio

Praise for

Far Better Money Management

"Joe Christian has written the ultimate guide to becoming a Do-It-Yourself investor. With excellent storytelling and powerful insights, you won't be able to put this book down."

—Marshall Goldsmith, world-renowned executive coach and author of *The New York Times* #1 bestsellers *Triggers*, *Mojo*, and *What Got You Here Won't Get You There*

"In Far Better Money Management, Joe demonstrates an insightful understanding of the human psyche that unblurs the lines between the world of money management and the poker table. There are the investor and the gambler, the patient and the anxious, the stoic and the emotional—all distinguishing traits that separate the winners from the losers. I have hired successful poker players as money managers, and I have witnessed many retired hedge fund managers go on to become successful poker players. There is often genius in simplicity, and this book is just that. The reader is furnished with the step-by-step guidance necessary to win the game of achieving financial independence. A fascinating read."

—Louis Bacon, Founder, Chairman, and principal investment manager, Moore Capital, a multibillion-dollar hedge fund

"Joe has written a gem of a book filled with fresh insights, cleverness, and humor. He also provides some interesting perspectives into our often-precarious relationship with money.
This book is both educational and entertaining!"

—**Deborah Price**, CEO and Founder, The Money Coaching Institute

"Humorous and instructive. Thank you for connecting the dots."

—**Michael Bologna**, Partner, NovaQuest Capital Management

"Who knew there could be a fascinating, engaging, and even gripping book about investing? Well, this is it. And it's a book about life. Short, punchy chapters will entertain you and give you plenty of guidance about the most important issues for prosperity and happiness. It's full of great stories and memorable quotes. I wish I had read this as a young man. Enjoy!"

—**Tom Morris**, bestselling author of *If Aristotle Ran General Motors, The Art of Achievement, Plato's Lemonade Stand,* and *The Oasis Within*, among many others

"Joe has written a fun, easy-to-read financial guide to life. I wish it had been required reading in college."

—**Munroe Cobey**, Retired Partner, Tudor Investment Corporation

"Joe Christian has demonstrated a great talent for storytelling. Making complex things simpler to understand cannot be underestimated when it comes to making significant changes. Changes for the better! Lots of fabulous nuggets of wisdom here!"

—**Joe Cross**, filmmaker, *Fat, Sick, and Nearly Dead*

"Insightful and provocative. With a unique gift for telling a good story, Joe engages the reader in such a way that the mystique of investing becomes a little less murky. THE perfect guide to becoming a Do-It-Yourself investor."

—**Mike Battistelli**, Founder, Alert Marketing Inc.

"Joe Christian has written a great financial book that will blow your mind. He has created a holistic plan to help you address any preconceived views you may have around money and expand those to guide you to achieve your wildest dreams. If you're looking to get out of debt and gain financial freedom, this book is for you."

—**Amanda Chay**, Founder, Wonderment Ltd.

To my three amazing daughters,

Emily, Hanna, and Grace.

Your love and support

fuel my passion more than you will ever know.

There is no greater wealth

than having you in my life.

Contents

Introduction

The only true wisdom is in knowing you know nothing.

—Socrates

Back in the summer of 1978, two incompletes shy of a Duke diploma and thoroughly sick of academia, I decided it was high time for an adventure. I somewhat forcibly enlisted a fraternity brother, loaded up my van with the essential requisites for that decade, and pointed it westward toward Las Vegas. I'm not sure he's ever forgiven me.

As we rolled into Vegas, my van decided it didn't appreciate the 115-degree welcome and retaliated by killing its water pump. One emergency repair and $100 later (basically a fortune back then), I figured I could make up for this unexpected inconvenience at the blackjack tables. After all, I was a math whiz replete with a so-called "sixth sense" for cards. Confidence? Sky-high.

Turns out, my skills were more myth than math. The brutal truth hit as I managed to triple my losses, effectively trading the cost of three water pumps for a lesson in humility. My bankroll depleted, I slunk out of Vegas, considerably poorer and a tad wiser.

Post-Vegas, a lightbulb went off. Maybe, just maybe, if I planned to gamble my hard-earned cash on blackjack, I should actually learn how to play effectively. Turns out, there's a right move for every card situation—hit, stand, split, you name it, all mapped out by endless computer simulations. This 'basic strategy' promises to shrink the house edge to less than 1 percent.

Armed with this newfound wisdom, I ventured back to Vegas years later. This time, not just to play, but to study the battlefield. It was almost painful watching folks blindly bet their mortgages on the turn of a card. If only they knew the fact that a few hours of strategic study could save their shirts.

These days, I steer clear of blackjack. The thrill of the gamble doesn't quite justify the perpetual edge in favor of the house. It's less about playing the game and more about playing the odds—something I've gotten quite good at, especially when it comes to managing money.

I might have initially overrated my blackjack abilities, but selling? That's something I've always had a knack for. Whether mowing lawns as a kid or solving complex financial situations as an adult, I've made a living out of talking folks into parting with their money. It's no surprise I wound up in financial services. After all, isn't playing the stock market just another high-stakes game, but with better odds if you know how to play your cards right?

Armed with a newly minted economics degree from Duke University (yes, I finally squared away those two incompletes), I swapped my van for a respectable car, bought a nice suit, retired my bong, got a haircut, and dove into the world of stock brokerage. Over the next thirty-two years, including running my own investment advisory company starting in 1996, I dedicated myself to the art of wealth management, helping clients to not just grow but also safeguard their wealth.

Starting out, I naively underestimated the sales aspect of the job. I thought I'd be diving straight into sophisticated financial strategizing—instead, I spent my days cold-calling prospects, trying to convince them that a greenhorn like me could manage their money better than brokers with decades of experience. That was a tough sell, but oddly enough, I loved it and thrived on the challenge.

But selling was only half the battle. Delivering on those promises was crucial; I needed to ensure my clients' financial growth to keep them from walking out the door. As emotions often clouded their financial decisions—like irrational bets placed at a blackjack table—I boned up on psychology, something I hadn't studied since my undergraduate years. This not only made me a better advisor but also a sharper salesman. In 2012, I sold my advisory business and shifted gears to coach executives and business owners to become more effective in their respective fields.

The finance world, laden with conflicts of interest, often places advisors' gains over clients' needs. I've navigated through decades of financial smoke and mirrors, and now, I aim to arm the average investor with the wisdom gleaned from my experiences.

This book is part of my mission to educate. It's a toolkit for achieving your financial goals and sidestepping the common traps that snag most investors. While experience is an excellent teacher, learning from others' mistakes can save you significant grief and expense. Whether you've already hit some financial milestones or are just starting to tackle your goals, this book will help you refine your strategy for a dignified retirement.

Retirement planning today is a stark contrast to the past—people once worked till sixty and passed by sixty-three, requiring minimal planning. Now, retirement can span decades, equaling the length of one's career, adding complexity to financial preparations.

On my journey from novice to expert, I've made some shrewd moves and a fair share of blunders. There's rich learning in those missteps, which I've compensated for over the years. Smart investing isn't as complex as the financial industry might have you believe—it's like blackjack, where a simple basic strategy can dramatically improve your odds. Many financial professionals, unfortunately, operate more like casino owners, complicating investing to justify their roles and fees.

As you embark on your financial journey, remember: the goal isn't just to manage money but to outlive it comfortably. Awareness of the industry's pitfalls can help you navigate this path more smoothly, ensuring that, in the end, your money outlasts you.

Back when I started my career, the internet was still a sci-fi fantasy, CNBC was non-existent, there was no stock ticker running across your TV screen, and the idea of discount brokers was laughable. Money magazine was barely finding its feet. The full-service broker reigned supreme, and we didn't hesitate to charge a whopping 2 percent on every stock trade—both coming and going. And mutual funds? We peddled those with hefty 8.5 percent commission. Oh, how times have changed! Now, trading commissions have plummeted to nearly zero and no-load mutual funds are ubiquitous.

Despite the plummeting costs, Wall Street is still kicking. Investment firms and their advisors are forever reinventing themselves, scrambling to justify their fees by promoting the latest financial cure-all. These days, it feels like there's a financial advisor on every corner promising riches. Even my auto insurance agent is after my IRA! I won't be surprised if my dry cleaner starts offering to trade options for me next week.

But let's be honest, the right investment path often isn't the stuff of thrilling cocktail party chatter. Tuning out the media buzz and ignoring Uncle Louie's "surefire" stock tip is usually a good bet. A little excitement here and there in your portfolio isn't bad—provided you understand what you're getting into.

Now, it's time to dive into an intelligent, unemotional, cost-effective investment strategy. In the next fifty-two chapters—call it a full deck—we'll tackle everything from mindset to knowledge to execution.

The Mindset Section is your crash course in the psychology of money. Brace yourself. It's time to become brutally honest about your financial behaviors and beliefs—some of which might be a bit outdated or downright wrong. This might feel like a therapy session, but it's crucial for laying the groundwork for effective financial planning.

The Knowledge Section sifts through the investment landscape to separate the wheat from the chaff. You'll come away with a clearer, big-picture view of your finances, perhaps even a few "aha" moments that challenge your previous assumptions.

The Execution Section translates that knowledge into action. It's like knowing the benefits of a healthy diet and exercise versus the dangers of smoking and junk food—knowing isn't enough without doing. Despite understanding what's good for them, people tend to fall short when it comes to execution, a consistent theme I've noticed throughout my coaching career.

Through engaging stories and accessible writing, I aim to keep you entertained while delivering solid financial advice. I frequently share about my experiences in Las Vegas and playing poker because the comparisons are stark and undeniable, particularly when it comes to rewiring your mindset. Don't be fooled by the light-hearted approach; this book is packed with practical insights. I've done the legwork of distilling complex investment concepts into something you can easily grasp and act on, so you can enjoy the benefits without getting bogged down in the details.

This book is like a treasure map to financial freedom, but remember, a map is only good if you're willing to follow it. I'm here to guide you from where you are to where you dream to be, financially speaking. However, it's crucial that you're not just a passive reader. Inaction is as good as stepping over dollars to pick up pennies. So, don't be that proverbial horse led to water but too stubborn to drink.

For the best results, I recommend reading this book from start to finish, resisting the temptation to skip straight to the juicy bits about knowledge and execution. There's no magic pill hidden in those later chapters that will suddenly make you wealthy. Trust me, if there were such a thing, I'd be on a yacht right now, not writing this book. You've got to take it step by step—crawl, walk, then run—and only after some serious financial fitness training should you even think about running that money marathon.

You might glance through the contents and think, "This doesn't apply to me." But even if not every single piece of advice fits your current situation, there's value in absorbing it all. Keep an open mind, toss out any old misconceptions about money, and prepare to be challenged.

By the end, you'll have the knowledge to take the reins of your financial future. Then, it all boils down to putting that knowledge into practice. Best of luck as you embark on this exciting financial journey—I'm rooting for you all the way!

MINDSET

1

The Essence
of Mindfulness

Until you make the unconscious conscious,
it will direct your life, and you will call it fate.

—Carl Jung

Ever noticed how top poker players remain cool under pressure? That's mindfulness in action. They're not just playing cards; they're playing their minds, staying present amidst the highs and lows. And guess what? Managing your money requires the same level of awareness.

Think of it like starting a twelve-step recovery program for your finances. The first step? Admitting that some of your financial strategies have been—let's be honest—a disaster. We've all been there, doing the same thing over and over and expecting a windfall the next time around. Spoiler alert: it doesn't work. Real progress starts with a change in mindset, recognizing that old tactics won't open new doors.

Our brains are wired with some pretty deep-rooted patterns. These subconscious beliefs can steer us wrong, mixing up fact and fiction and leading us down paths we didn't intend to take. If you find yourself driven by unexamined beliefs, then you're not in the driver's seat—autopilot is. And autopilot is oblivious to the realities of today's economy.

It's crucial to understand that past financial missteps don't need to dictate your future. There's always room to adjust the sails and chart a course toward financial stability—many have done it, and so can you. Whether you grew up in a financially savvy household or one where money was a constant struggle, each background presents unique challenges. If you're wondering whether you control your money or it controls you, it might be time for some reflection. And for those who have had to invent their own financial rulebook to compensate for a lack of guidance, consider whether your financial facade might be hiding a pile of debt.

If you're young and just starting out, consider yourself fortunate. Your slate isn't fully written on yet, and that's an advantage. Use this time to learn healthy financial habits before bad ones take root.

In essence, mindfulness in finance is about seeing clearly—your habits, your fears, and your real needs—so you can make choices that genuinely enrich your life, rather than chaining yourself to endless cycles of earning and spending. It's about making your money a tool for living well, not a measure of your worth.

Oh, how I wish this book had been around in my reckless twenties!

Money talks, but are we listening? No matter your walk of life or how savvy you think you are with your finances, there's always room for improvement. Some financial truths are timeless, yet others might just need a revision now and then. What worked for your grandparents might not get you through today's economic jungle.

As the years roll on, the financial priorities of your youth will inevitably shift. One day, the retirement you thought was ages away might knock on your door sooner than expected. Life has a knack for throwing curveballs—like an unexpected health issue or a sudden job loss—that could derail your financial stability. It's nearly guaranteed that life will surprise you with expenses you never planned for, so why not prepare for those surprises?

The first step is having those tough, honest talks about money. Remember, money is merely a tool, not the treasure chest itself. Waking up in a cold sweat worrying about finances is no way to live. Instead of stressing over how to hoard more cash, focus on strategies to make your money work for you. It's about creating a life you can enjoy without money worries nipping at your heels.

To kick things off, take a hard look at your past financial decisions— where have they led you? Scribble down some thoughts about your relationship with money. What's worked? What's flopped? Identifying these can help you forge a better path forward.

2

To Thine
Own Self Be True

Sometimes in order to be happy in the present moment,
you have to be willing to give up all hope for a better past.

—Robert Holden, PhD

Let's face it—we all make mistakes. My twenties were a parade of missteps, despite having all the ingredients for success: a shiny economics degree from Duke, a charming personality, and a brain sharper than a tack. I landed a great first job as a financial advisor and seemed set for life. But I had a major hiccup: a love affair with alcohol.

I won't drag you through the gory details of my misadventures, but let's just say my financial strategies were as wobbly as my walk home. I prioritized my needs over my clients', trusting me with money was like giving a toddler a porcelain vase—something was bound to break. Despite earning more than most, I spent even more, racking up a mountain of debt that made every breath a struggle.

It was a nightmare. As I spiraled down, I hit a crucial turning point on July 20, 1986—I quit drinking. Asking me then if I could skip booze for a year was like asking if I could dunk on Michael Jordan.

Improbable, right? But here I am, decades sober. Miracles do happen, folks.

My sobriety isn't a badge of pride but a token of gratitude. I'm truly one of the lucky ones who learned to live in the present because, honestly, you can't edit the past and the future's an open book. This realization revolutionized how I approached everything, including goal setting. I learned the art of living one day at a time and started crafting simple, clear daily plans that kept me grounded.

This transformation required that I adopt a level of brutal self-honesty that was unfamiliar territory in my experience. After years of self-deception, changing wasn't overnight. I revamped my approach to financial advising to align with my new mantra: honesty, integrity, and recommending to clients only what I'd do myself were I in their shoes. Initially, this meant leaving money on the table, but integrity paid off in the long run.

Why share this in a finance book? Because genuine financial planning begins with unflinching self-honesty. And it's never too late for a change.

Similarly, mastering blackjack meant ditching my naïveté and learning the real game. Once I did, I found smarter ways to invest my money. Whether you're facing retirement unequipped or living paycheck to paycheck, ignoring your financial fears won't make them disappear.

Start by vividly imagining your future. Have fun with it—create a vision board if that helps! There are no wrong answers here. If you're part of a duo, involve your partner to ensure you're aligned in your financial journey.

Change might seem just around the corner, but it's often a long road. I've walked it and guided many others down it as well. If you've lost your self-esteem, I assure you, it's recoverable. But you'll need to roll up your sleeves and dig deep. This book aims to be a tool in your journey of change.

Ask yourself: What lies have I believed? How would it feel to embrace radical honesty? Remember, change begins the moment you start being truthful with yourself.

3

Empowering Clarity

"Would you tell me, please, which way I ought to go from here?"
"That depends a good deal on where you want to get to," said the Cat.
"I don't much care where—" said Alice.
"Then it doesn't matter which way you go," said the Cat.
"—so long as I get SOMEWHERE," Alice added as an explanation.
"Oh, you're sure to do that," said the Cat, "if you only walk long enough."

—Lewis Carroll, from *Alice's Adventures in Wonderland*

Setting goals is something we've all dabbled in, whether it's losing a few pounds, kicking the nicotine habit, or trying to boost our bank accounts. Sometimes, we even surprise ourselves and actually succeed. But why is hitting these targets so darn hard? Often, it boils down to a lack of clarity. After all, if your goal is as vague as a foggy morning in San Francisco, you're likely not getting anywhere fast.

There is much to be learned from Thomas J. Watson, the founder of IBM. He's the guy who had a crystal-clear vision of IBM as a major player long before it was anything more than a few dusty desks in a dark office. He believed that to be a great company, you had to act like one from the start. It's like being the captain of a ship in a storm; Watson kept a keen eye on the gap between the IBM he had and the IBM he wanted, making constant adjustments to stay on course.

If you want to succeed at anything, you need to nail down what that "anything" is. Start by asking the hard questions: Why do you care about this goal? If it doesn't spark much interest, chances are you won't get very far chasing it.

Remember, if you don't know where you're heading, any road will do. What are your financial goals? Saving for retirement, a house, college, or perhaps a grand wedding? Pin down when you'd like these dreams to turn into reality. How about leaving something behind for the kids or charity? Calculate how much cash you'll need and set a deadline. This book isn't just going to help you do that—it's going to make it as easy as pie.

To pull off a solid financial plan, you need clarity because with clarity comes conviction. On a personal note, where do you see yourself living out your golden years? Are you globe-trotting or home gardening? Whatever your vision, write it down. Trust me, there's something magical about putting pen to paper—the more detailed, the better.

As your money mentor, I'm here to help you define these visions, map out a plan, and hold you accountable. We'll start with setting long-term goals that are as measurable as they are ambitious. A goal without a deadline is just a daydream. From there, we break it down: five-year goals, annual goals, monthly goals, all the way to daily objectives.

Here's a peek at my current daily checklist, which might inspire you to create yours:

1. Get eight hours of sleep.

2. Write for at least an hour.

3. Meditate.

4. Stretch or exercise.

5. Skip the sugar.

6. Be prudent with expenditures.

7. Study Spanish.

8. Read for an hour.

9. Keep TV time to an hour or less.

10. Do something thoughtful for someone else.

This might look like a simple to-do list, but sticking to these daily goals keeps me focused on what matters most to me. Scoring a perfect ten is rare, but oh, the thrill when it happens! I encourage my clients to craft their checklists too—it's always a blast to hear how they scored the previous day.

So, what's fuzzy in your life right now? Imagine having a clear plan. Picture how it feels knowing exactly where you're heading. Get those goals down on paper, set deadlines, and outline the steps you need to take. It's the first step towards turning your plans into reality.

4

Redefining Wealth

It's good to have money and the things that money can buy,
but it's good, too,
to check up once in a while and make sure
you haven't lost the things that money can't buy.

—George Lorimer

The 1980s was a wild time to be a stockbroker, a time when yuppies ruled, and the almighty dollar was king. I was there, raking it in and living the dream—or so I thought. My plan? Make a million by thirty, marry a trophy wife, and settle down with kids. Well, I scored the wife early, had a beautiful daughter, and... became a bankrupt alcoholic. So much for plans.

That rock-bottom moment led to a realization: there had to be more to life than just making money. I was smart, hardworking, and now sober. It was time to use those traits for good, not just my own gain.

Money means different things to different people, and you get to decide what it means for you. I used to be fascinated by discussions on who's richer or poorer until I realized I have better things to do than listening to endless bragging or complaining.

We often equate wealth with visible signs of affluence—mansions, fancy cars, designer clothes. But is that real wealth? Once upon a time, I thought so. But as I've grown older (and hopefully wiser), I've started to question that notion. I've managed money for "wealthy" folks who were downright miserable and known folks who barely made ends meet yet led joyously meaningful lives. An old friend once said success for him meant being able to fly first class or eat anywhere without worrying about the bill. If that's what makes you happy, who am I to judge?

Over the years, my definition of wealth has evolved. For me, it's about having the freedom to do what I want, when I want, without fretting over the price tag. The less I worry about money, the happier I am.

Of course, money is essential—we need it for the basics like food and shelter. It's hard to feel joyful if you're struggling to meet these needs. Relying on others when you're capable of providing for yourself isn't just unfair; it's downright embarrassing. Money isn't evil—it's necessary. It's what you do with it and how you let it shape your life that matters.

For me, the greatest achievement isn't in the bank balance I've grown but in raising three wonderful daughters who are each carving their own successful paths. No amount of money can top the pride I feel for them. But that's my view. What's yours?

Think about it—how would it feel to worry less about money and spend more time living? Take a moment to define what wealth means to you, on your own terms.

5

The
Loyalty
of Money

*I'm thankful for the three-ounce Ziploc bag
so I have somewhere to put my savings.*

—Paula Poundstone

Let me tell you about Archie Karas, possibly the most flamboyant cautionary tale Las Vegas has ever seen. Archie arrived in the U.S. from Greece with pockets as empty as his dreams were big. Starting as a waiter and a pool hustler, he quickly found his calling in poker, amassing $2 million. But faster than you can say "bad bet," it was gone. Not one to fold, Archie borrowed $10,000, turned it into $30,000, and after settling his debt, rampaged through pool halls and poker rooms to grow his stash to a staggering $40 million.

Now, with a fortune in hand, Archie sought advice from Lyle Berman, a poker legend and savvy businessman, who suggested buying an immediate annuity to secure a $200,000 monthly income without touching the $40 million principal. However, upon hearing it was taxable, Archie balked at the idea. Fast forward two years: every penny had vanished into the Vegas vortex, and Archie was back checking coats at the Golden Nugget.

While most of us won't sway with the financial gusto of Archie Karas, we all know someone who just can't seem to hang onto money, regardless of their income. From lottery winners to pro athletes, many who land sudden fortunes end up with nothing but a pile of debts and regrets. Why? Often, it's because they view money only as something to spend, not something to grow.

Take, for instance, a former employee of mine who, along with her husband, blew a $100,000 inheritance on matching Hummers. No thought for maintenance costs, taxes, or even fuel. They could've bolstered their retirement significantly but chose short-lived fame in their small town instead. Their financial strategy was as poorly planned as their vehicle choice was ostentatious.

Contrast this with the likes of Larry Fitzgerald, an NFL star with a penchant for practicality and a net worth nearing $100 million. Larry's approach? Spend on assets that appreciate. It's a simple strategy, but evidently, simplicity is genius.

The difference between financial fumbles and fortune often comes down to mindset. Those who succeed in the money game aren't necessarily the ones who make the most but rather those who manage it wisely. They save and invest consistently, eschewing flashy expenditures for smarter, value-appreciating purchases.

If you're pondering how to handle potential windfalls or just aiming not to be undone by your next paycheck, consider this: It's time to change how you think about and handle money. Reflect on how much money you've seen slip through your fingers. What portion have you saved? How would you manage a sudden financial boon?

If money has always felt more like sand slipping through your fingers than glue sticking to your hands, decide now to change. Start thinking of money as a tool not just for spending, but for making more money. It's time to get sticky with your finances.

6

Simplicity and Prosperity: Meet Beans

A man is rich in proportion to the number of things he can let alone.

—Henry David Thoreau

Back in the '80s, when I was a stockbroker, cold calling was the game, and I was a player. Imagine me dialing up folks with the big paychecks and bigger homes, trying to sell them the hottest stocks before we even had caller ID to dodge.

One memorable response came from a man intriguingly named Beans from a sleepy town in eastern North Carolina. He intrigued me with talk of a $30,000 investment—a hefty sum that could net me a cool $1,000 in commission. With dollar signs in my eyes, I set off for what I imagined might be Mayberry.

Pulling up to Beans' address, I thought I'd been pranked. The house looked more like a yard sale venue than an investor's residence, complete with tacky lawn ornaments and a rust-bucket car on blocks. But, having driven over two hours, I knocked on the door, met by an elderly man in a beer-stained tee and jeans offering me a Black Label beer—it was a far cry from a Heineken, but when in Rome, or rural North Carolina...

Beans and his wife were as down-to-earth as their decor. Midway through my pitch, Beans revealed their financials, and I almost choked on my budget beer. Between them, they had socked away almost $2.2 million in savings and stocks—on a janitor's and a clerk's salaries, no less.

Their secret? Any raise they ever got went straight to the bank or into company stock. No splurging on bigger homes or flashier cars. This unassuming couple had quietly amassed a fortune simply by living within their means and steadily investing the surplus.

It was a lesson in financial prudence right out of a storybook. Here I was, chasing high commissions and fancy beers, while Beans and his wife sat on a small fortune in a modest ranch house, completely content.

This encounter got me thinking wealth isn't about the size of your house or the brand of your car. It's about the peace that comes from financial security. Beans and his wife had it figured out—they understood something profound about true wealth.

So, what can we learn from Beans? Maybe it's that you don't need a flashy income to retire comfortably. Even a modest paycheck can turn into a million, given time and thrift. And perhaps most importantly, wealth might just be about knowing when enough is enough, which might mean swapping a Heineken for a Black Label every once in a while.

7

Cultivating Good Habits

People do not decide their futures; they decide their habits,
and their habits decide their future.

—F. M. Alexander

It's time to take a hard look at your habits—the good, the bad, and the ugly—and consider which ones you might want to ditch, tweak, or totally overhaul. Think of it as housekeeping for your behavioral closet.

Habits, much like compound interest, build over time—great for the good ones, not so much for the ones that lead you astray. Take starting a new workout regime, for instance. You won't see those six-pack abs overnight, but stay the course, and the results will come. Similarly, if you're trying to eat healthier, maybe give those supermarket donuts a pass next time. Trust me, your waistline will thank you later.

Back in my early poker-playing days, I had a bad habit of bluffing just for the thrill of it. Sure, it was a rush to see seasoned players fold under my audacious bets, but it was a fast track to losing money. Lesson learned? Identify the bad habits, then boot them out.

We're all creatures of habit and flipping a bad habit into a good one can be simpler than you think. For instance, instead of focusing on not hitting the ball into the woods when I golf, I visualize it landing perfectly on the fairway. Positive visualization works wonders, and not just in sports.

If you're looking to whip your finances into shape, start by jotting down your current financial habits—the good, the bad, and the maybe not so ugly. Recognizing them is the first step toward change.

Procrastination is a common nemesis, and it's easy to justify putting things off in the moment. But, as we all know, delaying often costs us more in the end. This is known as present bias, where the immediate pleasures overshadow the long-term gains, like that new car smell that makes us forget about the hefty monthly payments that follow.

One effective way to combat procrastination and other detrimental habits is not through sheer willpower but by setting up systems. Systems create a framework that helps ensure what needs to get done, gets done. It's about simplifying your life, not complicating it.

For example, consider implementing a time-blocking system. Dedicate a couple of hours each month to sit down uninterrupted and manage your finances. It's a simple but powerful habit that can have a profound impact on your financial health.

Remember, focusing on the process rather than the outcome allows for more manageable, consistent actions that lead to results over time. Start small, think big, and let the habits you cultivate pave the way to a future you've not just dreamed of but planned for.

Where have your habits taken you off course? What new habits could you introduce to steer back in the right direction? Sometimes, the thrill of conquering your impulses offers the best kind of instant gratification.

8

The Temptation of Now

Because money permits a constant stream of luxuries and indulgences, it can take away their savor, and by permitting instant gratification, money shortcuts the happiness of anticipation.
Scrimping, saving, imagining, planning, hoping—these stages enlarge the happiness we feel.

—Gretchen Rubin

In poker and life, the thrill of the immediate can be your worst enemy. Just like rookie poker players who can't wait for the right hand and push their chips in too early, many of us fall for the siren song of instant gratification. We want the rush now, forgetting that the big wins often come to those who wait.

Take the famous Stanford marshmallow experiment. Kids were given a choice: one marshmallow now, or two if they could wait fifteen minutes. The kids who waited not only got more treats, but they also grew up to have higher SAT scores, better health, and generally more successful lives. It turns out, being able to delay gratification is a pretty good predictor of future success.

Now, think about your own "marshmallow moments." Ever by-passed adding to your savings because that shiny new gadget caught your eye? We've all been there. But every time we give in to the impulse purchase, we chip away at our long-term financial health. It's not just about self-control; it's about understanding the trade-offs we're making.

Most Americans will bring in enough money over their lifetimes to secure a comfortable retirement. Yet, bombarded by a culture of now, we're tempted daily to splurge on things we're convinced will make us happy. Spoiler alert: that happiness is usually short-lived.

Want to break the cycle of instant gratification? Here's how you can start:

- **Prioritize What Matters:** Figure out what's truly important to you and align your spending with those values.

- **Set Clear Goals:** Know what you want to achieve and plot a course to get there.

- **Recognize Trade-Offs:** Every dollar spent now is a dollar you won't have later.

- **Resist Impulses:** Avoid making purchases on a whim.

- **Choose Wisely:** Make decisions that favor your future needs over present wants.

I'm not saying turn into a miser who never enjoys the fruits of their labor. Just consider being a bit more thoughtful about your choices. You may be surprised by how little you need to give up to meet your financial goals. And when you do hit those milestones, go ahead and treat yourself. Celebrating your victories is part of the journey.

Reflect on this: How has giving in to immediate gratification shaped your current financial landscape? Imagine where you could be if you had often opted to wait. The small sacrifices now could lead to a richer and more fulfilling life later. Remember, the long-term consequences of short-term behaviors are real and can be profound.

9

Paper or Plastic?

Actions speak louder than words and not nearly as often.

—Mark Twain

Like most folks, you probably carry a small arsenal of payment options in your wallet. Sure, credit cards are handy, but do you really need an entire deck of them? They can make spending dangerously easy.

Consider this: casinos don't use cash at the tables—they use chips. There's a good reason for that. It's much easier to bet with a $100 chip than a $100 bill because once that money converts into chips, it doesn't feel like real money anymore. Most folks end up gambling it all rather than cashing out what's left, which, by the way, requires finding the cashier—a journey comparable to a quest for the Holy Grail, especially after a few complimentary cocktails. This detachment from the real value of money is exactly what happens when you swipe your card instead of handing over cold, hard cash.

If you suspect a spending problem is barricading the path to your financial goals, it's time to get real about your habits. Try using cash for everything for a couple of weeks. Feel the pain and the pleasure of handing over actual money. You'll likely think twice about that daily designer coffee when you physically see your wallet thinning.

This cash-only trial might just teach you a thing or two about the ease with which you part with your money.

My kids think it's hilarious that I still use cash for small purchases. So many of the younger generation never seem to have actual money in their pockets, but they're never short of plastic. They are perpetually shocked by their monthly credit card statements, which inevitably prompt the classic, "I spent how much?" Thankfully, for them, there's always the minimum payment option.

I'm well aware that cash is on its way to becoming a relic. One day, we'll likely pay for everything digitally. But for now, I enjoy being a holdout, the last of a dying breed. Plus, it gives my kids a good chuckle.

Don't get me wrong, I don't despise credit cards. In the realm of online shopping, they're practically a necessity, offering more fraud protection than debit cards. Plus, many cards provide perks like cash back or travel miles, which are great—as long as they don't tempt you to spend foolishly. "Free is free," after all.

Yet, simplicity has its virtues. Try sticking to one or two credit cards. It's easier to track, and simpler to manage your spending. If you're a business owner, consider a separate card for business expenses only. Pay off the balance each month and live within your means.

Both credit and debit cards offer another benefit: an electronic record of your expenses, great for tracking and tax purposes. Debit cards are especially good for small, local purchases since they cost vendors less to process.

So, what's your credit card strategy? Are you the pay-off-full-balance monthly type, or is debt creeping up on you? Maybe it's time to review your credit card collection and snip the excess.

Why not challenge yourself to a cash-only week? It could be just what you need to reset your spending habits. Pay attention to where your money goes—it might just surprise you how much more you value it when you feel every dollar leave your hand

10

Not Just
a River in Egypt

Most men would rather deny a hard truth than face it.

—George R. R. Martin

Denial isn't just a river in Egypt; it's often a block in our financial journey. Recognizing bad money habits is one thing; admitting you're in denial about them is another level entirely. This denial can be a huge roadblock to financial success.

Think about the alcoholic or addict whose recovery hinges on admitting there's a problem. As they learn in twelve-step programs, acknowledging the issue is the critical first step. I often find myself reciting the Serenity Prayer out loud—" God, grant me the serenity to accept the things I cannot change, courage to change the things I can, and wisdom to know the difference." It's short, sweet, and hits hard—perfect for financial recovery too.

Let's face it, some people are dealt a better hand in life. They're born into wealth, intelligence, and stability. Others find themselves in tougher circumstances that breed dependency and blame. However, no matter the starting point, the trajectory of our lives often boils down to the choices we make. You can't rewrite your past, but you can learn from it and make better choices moving forward.

Failures? We've all had our share. And sure, it's tempting to sweep them under the rug to avoid embarrassment or pain. But remember what Thomas Edison said about his "failures" when inventing the lightbulb? They weren't failures; they were simply steps on the path to success. That's the mindset of a winner.

In poker, it's not about the cards you're dealt but how you play them. Height, weight, speed—none of that matters at the poker table. It's all about strategy. When Chris Moneymaker turned an $86 online poker entry into $2.5 million at the 2003 World Series of Poker, he didn't just win a game; he changed the game. It showed that anyone with the right moves could achieve financial freedom.

We're all in denial about something. Gamblers boast about their wins and forget their losses as if they never happened. The best strategy against denial? Recognize it, acknowledge it, and move on. Laugh at yourself a bit.

Ignoring a problem doesn't make it disappear. I've seen people grocery shop with food stamps at convenience stores—now that's not stretching your dollar. Meanwhile, seemingly affluent folks can often be spotted bargain hunting at Dollar Tree or stocking up at Costco. Shifting some spending habits to free up cash for investments might require you to skip buying that new car to keep pace with the one your neighbor just flaunted.

Financial prosperity is within reach for anyone willing to take an honest look at their money habits and make necessary changes. Most people would rather listen to nails on a chalkboard than scrutinize their financial habits, but understanding and addressing these habits is key to improvement.

So, where are you in denial? What might change if you faced this head-on? Acknowledging and addressing how denial affects your finances is not just freeing; it's financially prudent. Decide where you stand, make the needed adjustments, and perhaps you'll find that addressing denial not only changes your finances but transforms your life.

11

Emotional Intelligence

The degree of one's emotions
varies inversely with one's knowledge of the facts.

—Bertrand Russell

Reflecting on the myriad of emotional decisions I've made about money, I can confidently say each was a recipe for regret. Emotions, those sneaky instigators of questionable choices, often lead us down paths we'd rather not travel. Ever tried to win back your losses in one grand gesture? There's a whole city thriving on that dream—hello, Las Vegas!

During my countless hours at the poker tables, I've learned that keeping your cool during a downturn is an art form. In poker, a 'bad beat' is when you lose despite holding a hand that was a statistical shoo-in. It stings, especially when there's serious cash on the line. The aftermath? Many players go on 'tilt,' a state of emotional frenzy that can derail even the most disciplined gambler, leading to decisions they'll later lament.

When it comes to investing, emotions are equally treacherous. In a bull market, it's easy to ride the wave of optimism, ignoring risks. But when the market takes a nosedive, that same optimism can turn into excessive caution, causing investors to pull back when they should be looking for opportunities. This emotional rollercoaster can make you feel invincible when prices are soaring and utterly defeated when they plummet—exactly the opposite of how savvy investors should react.

Not every investment will be a blockbuster hit like Apple or Amazon. Even the most well-researched bets can flop. The key is not letting your emotions dictate your actions when they do. Emotional investing often compels selling low and buying high—the exact opposite of a profitable strategy.

Later chapters will detail investment strategies designed to minimize emotional involvement by sticking to a systematic approach. This method helps keep the emotional gremlins at bay.

If you find yourself clouded by emotional fog, it might be time to 'get up from the table.' Don't chase after losses by throwing good money after bad. Adopting a stoic approach during these testing times can lead to substantial long-term gains.

Now, think back. What financial decisions have you made while under emotional distress? How can you prevent a future tilt? Remember, in the arena of investing, emotions should be left at the door.

12

The Herd Mentality Trap

The whole problem with the world is that fools and fanatics are always so certain of themselves, and wiser people so full of doubts.

—Bertrand Russell

The pull of the herd is strong. Throughout history, the madness of crowds has had a major role in some of the most spectacular financial fiascos. From tulip mania in the 17th century, where people traded homes for flower bulbs, to the dot-com bubble and the more recent real estate collapse—humans have a knack for rushing in where angels fear to tread.

Remember Charles Ponzi? He promised a 50% return in just 45 days to his fellow Italian immigrants in the 1920s. It didn't end well, turning his last name into financial jargon for fraud. Then there's Bernie Madoff, who might as well have been named Bernie "Made-off" with all that money, thanks to his Ponzi scheme that duped even the savviest investors.

And who could forget the Nigerian prince emails? I was promised a hefty fee to help bring millions into the U.S. The prince is still waiting on my reply.

But here's the kicker: these scams endure because people keep falling for them. It's the lure of the quick buck, the easy payout, which ensnares so many.

The late '90s brought us the dot-com bubble, fueled by wild speculation in tech stocks. Prices soared, confidence bubbled over, and traditional investment wisdom was thrown out the window. The bubble burst when the tech-heavy Nasdaq took a nosedive from its peak in March 2000.

Fast forward to 2007, and the same song played with a real estate twist. Everyone agreed real estate was a sure bet—until it wasn't. Mortgage lenders handed out loans like candy at a parade, assuming ever-rising home prices would cover any risk. When the bubble popped, the financial fallout was monumental.

Economist Robert Schiller described this phenomenon as "irrational exuberance," a product of human psychology where the fear of missing out (FOMO) drives people to jump on the bandwagon. Even those who suspect they're making a shaky investment often drag their friends along, hoping there's safety in numbers.

We've all been there—tempted to follow the crowd because FOMO is a powerful motivator. If everyone around you is on their feet clapping, chances are you'll stand up too, even if you thought the performance was mediocre. Manias create bubbles, and bubbles always burst. Remember, if it sounds too good to be true, it probably is.

So, what can you do with this history lesson? How do you avoid getting swept up in the next big financial delusion? Here's the plan: I'll show you a practical investment strategy that sidesteps the pitfalls of groupthink.

Reflect on these questions:

- When has FOMO led you astray in your financial decisions?

- Have you ever been burned by an investment that promised the moon?

- Next time you hear about a "sure thing," will you greet it with skepticism?

If an investment smells fishy, it's probably not your next gourmet dinner—it's likely a day-old tuna sandwich. Run the other way.

13

Challenging Conventional Wisdom

Believe nothing, O monks, merely because you have been told it . . .
or because it is traditional, or because you yourselves have imagined it.
Do not believe what your teacher tells you merely out of respect for the
teacher. But whatsoever, after due examination and analysis, you find
to be conducive to the good, the benefit, the welfare of all beings—that
doctrine believe and cling to and take it as your guide.

—Gautama Buddha

The annals of history are littered with "experts" who got it spectac-
ularly wrong. "Who the hell wants to hear actors talk?" pondered
H. M. Warner of Warner Brothers in 1927. Fast forward, and silent
films are a niche art form at best. Then there's Ken Olsen, founder
of Digital Equipment, who in 1977 famously declared, "There is no
reason anyone would want a computer in their home." Oh, Ken, if
only you could see us now.

These blunders highlight a crucial point: clinging to prevailing wisdom can be the quickest path to missing out on the next big thing. Consider Fred Smith, the mind behind FedEx, whose college professor scoffed at his idea of a reliable overnight delivery service, or Steve Jobs, who faced rejection from Atari and Hewlett-Packard when seeking early funding.

What about the so-called financial wisdom we hear bandied about? "Owning your own home is the cornerstone of achieving the American dream." Perhaps. There's the often-cited mantra, "A loss on paper is not a loss until you sell." Comforting, yet potentially misleading. And who hasn't heard, "You can't go wrong taking a profit"? That might soothe the soul unless you sold Apple shares shortly after their IPO for a tidy profit, missing out on a windfall as those shares skyrocketed in value decades later—like yours truly did.

And let's not forget the gold enthusiasts, proclaiming it the ultimate hedge against both inflation and deflation. The logic there still ties my brain in knots. Just because a belief is popular doesn't make it foolproof.

It's crucial to question the status quo. Healthy skepticism and a dash of common sense are invaluable. Remember, just because everyone thinks something is a great idea doesn't necessarily mean it is. Reflect on the times when widely accepted beliefs in your life turned out to be myths.

Are you prepared to accept that prevailing wisdom might not always be right? Can you stand apart from the crowd and make independent decisions? Embrace the questions more than the answers; they often lead to deeper insights and better decisions.

14

The Fallacy of Sunk Cost

The past is a great place,
and I don't want to erase it or to regret it,
but I don't want to be its prisoner either.

—Mick Jagger

Ever found yourself halfway through a movie so terrible that even the popcorn starts to taste bad, yet you stick it out because, well, you've already wasted an hour so you might as well finish? Or perhaps you've dutifully cleaned off a plate at a restaurant not because you were enjoying the meal, but simply because you paid for it. These are classic examples of succumbing to the sunk cost fallacy, where you continue a futile action because you feel that you've invested too much to quit.

This flawed thinking isn't just about wasting time on bad movies or overeating. It extends to more significant decisions like investments, where it can do real damage. In poker, for example, players often throw good money after bad, compelled by the amount they've already bet rather than the poor odds of winning more. Similarly, investors might hold onto plummeting stocks because they can't bear to realize a loss, hoping against hope that things will turn around.

Consider the roulette wheel. If black has come up five times in a row, betting everything on red because "it's due" doesn't change the odds that black could come up yet again. The roulette ball has no memory; it doesn't care. Likewise, a stock doesn't know you own it, what you paid for it, and won't perform better just to please you.

Recognizing sunk costs and learning to ignore them can lead to more rational decisions. If a course of action isn't working, sometimes the wisest choice is to cut your losses and move on, rather than doubling down on a failing strategy.

For instance, think about an investment property that requires more time and effort than the returns justify. If you wouldn't buy it at its current market price knowing what you now know, why hold onto it? This was the case with a friend who owned a beach house. It seemed like a great idea until she realized it was netting her a measly return and could potentially slide into the red with one bad rental season or a natural disaster. Despite the emotional tug to hang onto it, selling turned out to be the smarter move.

The next time you catch yourself justifying continued investment in a losing proposition, whether it's stock, real estate, or even a pair of painfully pinching shoes, ask yourself: If I weren't already involved, would I want in now? If the answer is no, it might be time to let go.

We've all faced sunk cost fallacies, making poor choices because we can't bear to see our initial investments go to waste. It's human nature. But by recognizing these moments, we can start making decisions based on the future value of things, rather than what we've already lost. After all, isn't it better to walk away from the past than to let it hobble your future? So, the next time sunk costs beckon, remember: Don't just sit there because you already paid for the ticket—walk out of the theater if you need to, and don't look back.

15

Adrenaline Junkies

Patience is bitter, but its fruit is sweet.

—Jean-Jacques Rousseau

Ask any pro poker player about the most common blunder amateurs make, and you'll likely hear how they play too many hands. Unlike the movies, where every hand is a heart-stopper, real winning poker is more of a slow dance. A seasoned cash player might be thrilled to scoop up just one or two significant pots an hour, using patience to cultivate a solid bankroll over time.

When the right cards do come along—which can sometimes feel like waiting for a comet to pass—pros pounce, leveraging favorable odds with a hefty bet. For amateurs, though, the waiting game can be torturous. Boredom and the itch for action often lead them to overplay a weak hand. It's like mistaking a mirage for an oasis; suddenly, those modest pocket fives look as good as aces, and that's when the trouble starts.

I've been there myself, mistaking patience for inactivity. After a dull couple of hours, even a marginal hand starts looking pretty good, and that's often where the problems begin. However, these hard-learned lessons aren't just about poker. They apply across the board, particularly in investing.

The world of investing isn't that different from a poker table. Think of it as a zero-sum game: for every investor counting their gains, there's someone tallying their losses. The casinos—aka the stock market—take their cut, and the game goes on. I've seen plenty of eager tourists at the poker tables, happy to churn their hard-earned cash for a few hours of thrill. They leave with lighter wallets, comforting themselves with the "entertainment value" of the experience. And, while they chalk up losses to fun, I'm more than happy to help lighten their load.

Investing should be equally methodical. The urge to make a quick buck can be overwhelming, but true gains are made slowly. Day trading? More like day gambling. If you know a day trader who's truly ahead in the long run, they're a rarer species than you might think. They remember every win with crystal clarity but somehow forget the losses—much like those casino goers.

Being an investor rather than a gambler means embracing boredom. Yes, the markets will swing; there will be highs and lows, booms and busts. But remember, in the classic fable, it wasn't the flashy hare that won the race—it was the steady, unassuming turtle.

So, ask yourself: Do you only recall your wins and conveniently forget the losses? Can you approach investing with a steady hand, unswayed by the siren song of quick profits? Are you prepared to be the investor equivalent of watching paint dry?

If you're looking for excitement, find it elsewhere—skydiving, spelunking, or spider wrangling—just keep it out of your portfolio. Investing isn't about adrenaline; it's about smart, boring choices that pay off in the long run.

16

Mindset Recap

When our knowing exceeds our sensing,
we will no longer be deceived by the illusion of our senses.

—Walter Russell

We've journeyed through a plethora of insights in these pages, and hopefully, I've hit a nerve or two (in a good way!) about how to better manage your finances. Here's a quick recap of what we've learned:

- **Study Before You Play**: Understand the rules thoroughly before diving into any financial endeavor.

- **Change Your Money Mindset**: Stop viewing money as a burden; start seeing it as a tool that can work for you.

- **Set Concrete Goals**: A goal unwritten or without a due date is a pipe dream.

- **Seek Honesty and Clarity**: Be honest with yourself about your finances; clarity is the first step to control.

- **Know Your Destination:** If you don't have a clear direction, any path will do. Define where you want to go financially.

- **Personalize Your Wealth:** Your definition of wealth is yours alone—customize it, don't crowdsource it.

- **Get Sticky With Money:** Like good glue, make sure your money sticks around.

- **Remember Beans:** You don't need a fortune to retire comfortably—you just need to be smart about what you have.

- **Consider the Long-Term:** Short-term decisions can have long-lasting impacts, so think about the future with every financial choice.

- **Resist Instant Gratification:** The lure of the immediate can be strong, but true rewards come from patience and persistence.

- **Monitor Your Spending:** Pay attention to where your money goes. Make an effort to invest in assets that appreciate, not depreciate.

- **Acknowledge Your Denial:** Recognize when you're in denial about your finances—it's a tricky beast that can sabotage your success.

- **Manage Your Emotions:** Keep a cool head. Emotions can skew financial decisions, often to your detriment.

- **Question the Consensus:** Just because everyone thinks it's a great idea, doesn't mean it is. Do your due diligence.

- **Take Prevailing Wisdom with Skepticism:** History is littered with the majority being wrong; don't be afraid to stand apart.

- **Avoid Sunk Cost Traps:** Don't let past investments dictate future decisions if they no longer make sense.

- **Patience Pays Off:** In investing, as in life, time is on your side. Use it wisely.

Feel free to come back to this chapter whenever you need a reminder of these core principles.

With the psychological groundwork laid, it's time to delve deeper into the financial landscape—the good, the bad, and the ugly—to truly prepare for your journey to financial freedom. Remember, it all starts with the right mindset.

KNOWLEDGE

17

Esse Quam Videri: Being Over Seeming

The way to gain a good reputation
is to endeavor to be what you desire to appear.

—Socrates

I consider myself a solid poker player, and a big part of my success comes from sizing up my fellow players. Are they just vacationers happy to gamble away their spending money for kicks? Are they cautious or throwing caution to the wind? Do they even know how to play? It's crucial to understand who's at your table, especially when the game is high stakes.

In the world of finance, if you're thinking about hiring a financial advisor, you'll notice many of them flaunt a string of impressive-sounding initials after their names. But what do these credentials really mean? Let's decode the most prestigious titles in the finance arena:

1. Chartered Financial Analyst (CFA):

Think of the CFA as the heavyweight champion of financial credentials. It's a beast to earn, requiring mastery of a broad range of topics from ethics to security analysis. Holders of this title typically work in high-level finance roles like managing big investment funds or crunching numbers at major banks.

2. Certified Financial Planner (CFP):

The CFP is your go-to for expertise in financial planning, including everything from taxes to retirement schemes. The rigorous training and ethical standards they adhere to mean they're committed to putting your interests first, making them a trustworthy partner in planning your financial future.

3. Chartered Institute of Management Accountant (CIMA):

Awarded by the Investments and Wealth Institute, the CIMA focuses on the art and science of building investment portfolios. It's not a quick study; earning this title is a marathon, not a sprint.

4. Certified Public Accountant (CPA):

The CPA is likely the most familiar to you. Specializing in taxes and accounting, CPAs are the folks you want on your side when the taxman comes. Achieving CPA status is tough and requires a serious knack for numbers.

Each of these credentials demands significant study and a series of tough exams. They're not just decorative—they signify a deep and committed understanding of their field.

Additionally, the Financial Industry Regulatory Authority (FINRA) regulates much of the licensing needed to actually practice selling financial products:

- **Series 7**: The all-access pass for financial advisors, allowing them to sell nearly any type of financial product. This is the big one, and earning it is no small feat.

- **Series 6**: This license lets advisors deal with mutual funds and other packaged investment products, but not individual stocks or bonds.

- **Series 63**: Required across the states, this certification ensures advisors are up to snuff on state laws and regulations.

- **Series 65**: Essential for advisors who charge fees for their advice rather than earning commissions on the sale of products.

Understanding these qualifications can help you choose an advisor who not only talks the talk but walks the walk. After all, in finance as in poker, it pays to know who's sitting at your table.

"Esse quam videri," meaning "to be rather than to seem," is more than just a lofty phrase—it's a vital approach when navigating the world of financial advice. The title "financial advisor" is widely used, but not all who wear this label are equipped with the credentials that really count.

Holding one or more respected licenses, such as the Series 7 or CFP, marks someone as a truly qualified financial advisor. Unfortunately, the financial industry is bustling with self-proclaimed experts whose credentials don't always stack up. While providing financial advice doesn't necessarily require a license, selling financial products does—though the specifics can vary based on the products and the method of compensation.

In recent years, there's been a concerning trend where life insurance agents sell index-linked financial products under the guise of being qualified advisors. These agents, licensed only to sell insurance, sometimes present themselves as equals to those holding Series 7 licenses, which is misleading. The extensive training and rigorous exams required for legitimate investment advisor licenses put these professionals on a different level entirely.

The waters are further muddied by a slew of dubious designations that are often little more than marketing tools. These credentials can be misleading, requiring minimal effort and no real mastery of the subject. They're designed to impress rather than educate, and it's crucial to recognize them for what they are.

Moreover, certain designations target vulnerable groups such as seniors, exploiting fears like outliving savings, or religious groups, attempting to blend faith with financial advice. Always scrutinize these closely. For example, the CFPN might sound similar to the well-respected CFP, but don't be fooled—look beyond the letters to the actual qualifications and regulatory standards.

When choosing a financial professional, it's crucial to delve deep into the meaning behind their credentials. Ask about the required study, the examination process, and ongoing education. Know what each set of initials stands for and the expertise it truly represents.

The bottom line? Don't just be swayed by a string of letters after a name. Ask pointed questions to understand whether these credentials align with your financial needs and goals. "To be rather than to seem" isn't just sage advice—it's a necessity when choosing who to trust with your financial future.

So, next time you meet a financial advisor, don't just nod appreciatively at their business card. Be prepared to ask the hard questions: What do those certifications really mean? How do they benefit you? Remember, in the realm of financial advice, appearances can be deceiving.

18

Talking Heads

I'd like to be known for more
than being the guy in the big suit.

—David Byrne

Just like David Byrne isn't just the guy in the big suit, good financial advice should be more than flashy talk. A seasoned poker player once enlightened me with the notion that players often overestimate their skills, much like they might their prowess in other areas of life. This humorous observation is alarmingly similar to how people perceive financial pundits.

Financial media is a bustling stage where everyone is vying for the spotlight, often serving their own interests rather than yours. It's a world where conflicts of interest are as common as bad bluffs at a poker table. Most financial advisors are often on the hunt for commissions, pushing products that may not always align with the client's best interests. Fortunately, the era of hefty commissions on every trade is dwindling, making room for fee-only advisors who tend to align more closely with client needs.

Turn on CNBC or Bloomberg, and you'll encounter a parade of experts who are more interested in raising their profile or managing more assets than in providing genuine, unbiased advice. These financial "experts" can have their moment of glory, accurately predicting market movements, but remember—even a broken clock is right twice a day. When the economy is booming, these analysts appear brilliant. When the market tanks, the same voices quickly morph into prophets of doom, conveniently forgetting their previous optimism.

This selective memory is not just amusing but telling. The financial media thrives on bull markets because high stakes and high interest equate to high ratings. This inherent bias towards optimism pervades the industry, often overshadowing more balanced or cautious perspectives.

If you find yourself constantly reacting to the advice of these talking heads, you might be playing a losing game. Financial media, for all its glitz and urgency, often leads to inefficient money management and poor investment choices. Markets naturally ebb and flow, influenced by countless factors, including political climates. Politicians, regardless of party, often claim credit for economic successes and disavow failures, but the truth is that market cycles are far more powerful than any single administration's policies.

While financial news plays a critical role in disseminating timely information, it's primarily a for-profit spectacle that caters to our love for drama—much like the Weather Channel's coverage of the "killer storms" that may or may not hit. We're drawn to the suspense, even when the threat is minimal.

So, take a step back and critically assess the motives behind the advice given by both the media and your financial advisor. Are their recommendations truly in your best interest, or are they just another part of the show? Remember, the more you meddle with your investments based on the latest media frenzy, the more likely you are to erode your wealth.

Have you ever been swayed by a slick presentation rather than solid advice? What costly mistakes have you made by listening to the market noise? Identifying where this noise infiltrates your financial decisions is the first step toward tuning it out.

Learning to maintain a stoic disposition in the face of market swings can ultimately turn volatility into opportunity. It's not just about surviving the storm—it's about thriving in it.

19

The Rake

It's not what you pay a man, but what he costs you that counts.

—Will Rogers

Let's talk about the house advantage, both in casinos and in the world of investing. Casinos are a masterclass in profitability. They invest in lavish décor and offer free drinks, but they still come out on top thanks to games designed to beat the average Joe over time. Your Uncle Louie's tall tales of striking it rich in Vegas? They're the exception, not the rule. Games like blackjack, roulette, and baccarat are tailored to ensure the house wins in the long run, thanks to the statistical magic of the law of large numbers.

Poker, however, plays by different rules. It's you against other players, not the house. So, how do casinos profit from poker? They take a rake—a small percentage of each pot, typically around 10% with a cap on each hand dealt. It's a subtle process, but over dozens of hands an hour, this translates into big, predictable earnings for the house, regardless of who wins or loses at the table.

In the investment world, we face our version of the rake. It's crucial to understand the fees and commissions tied to your investments because, like the rake in poker, they can chip away at your returns. Sure, there are low-cost investment options out there, but remember:

being penny-wise can sometimes lead you to be pound-foolish. It's easy to overlook the value of seasoned advice in the rush to cut costs.

If you're a DIY investor, by all means, embrace low-cost strategies to maximize your returns. But if you're among the many who value guidance, demand clarity about the fees you're paying and ensure you're getting good value for your money.

Remember, there's nothing inherently wrong with advisors charging fees—that's how they make their living. But you should be vigilant. Some investment products, especially certain insurance investments and mutual funds, can be structured to hide their true costs through back-end fees and hefty surrender charges if you withdraw funds too early.

Beware the old "no commission" pitch. It's often a sleight of hand where the advisor is paid upfront by the product provider. In the world of finance, just like in a casino, there's no such thing as a free lunch. Every cost, whether upfront or hidden in the fine print, comes from your wallet and impacts your investment's growth potential.

Consider this math: $100,000 invested at an 8% annual return grows to $1,006,266 in thirty years. But slice off a 1% management fee and compound annually at 7% instead, and you're looking at $761,226—a stark $245,040 less! Ask yourself, is it worth learning to manage your investments to save that kind of cash? I'd say so.

So, as you navigate your financial journey, ask the critical questions:

- How much are you really paying for financial advice?
- What exactly are you getting in return?
- Is it time to take more control over your financial decisions?

Remember, every penny you save on fees is a penny that can grow over time.

20

Twenty Questions

He who asks a question remains a fool for five minutes;
he who does not ask a question remains a fool forever.

—Chinese proverb

It's a curious truth: many folks will spend more time planning a weeklong vacation than plotting out their decades-long retirement. If you're on the brink of choosing a financial advisor, or rethinking your current one, roll up your sleeves—it's question time.

The world is teeming with so-called financial "experts," sporting titles like estate planner or investment counselor. In my experience, only a select few truly have the chops to effectively guard and grow your wealth.

Don't shy away from interviewing potential advisors. A rigorous Q&A can lay the foundation for a partnership that lasts a lifetime. Here's your cheat sheet to get started:

1. What's your educational background?

2. How long have you been doling out financial advice?

3. Are you flying solo, or are you part of a larger firm?

4. What's your investment philosophy?

5. How do you earn your keep?

6. What investment products do you typically use?

7. Who's your average client, and what are their goals?

8. What licenses and certifications have you earned?

9. Do you offer financial planning services, and is there a charge?

10. How often do you meet with clients?

11. What kind of performance reports do you provide?

12. What's your approach in a bull market?

13. And in a bear market?

14. Do you have discretionary trading authority?

15. How do you research investment opportunities?

16. What do you consider a "good" return?

17. How long do you plan to stay in business?

18. What happens if something happens to you?

19. What justifies your fees?

20. Can you share references from long-term clients with similar goals to mine?

Schedule a face-to-face meeting and pop these questions unexpectedly. You're not just checking their knowledge but also their ability to handle pressure. The best advisors stay cool when under the spotlight; those who stumble or seem evasive are red flags.

Remember, this isn't just about feeling informed—it's about ensuring that your financial future is in capable hands. Make sure every one of your questions is answered thoroughly before you move forward.

Are you ready to ask these questions? Imagine the peace of mind you'll have, knowing you've thoroughly vetted the person handling your financial future. Isn't that worth a bit of homework?

21

What Is Stock Anyway?

Investing should be more like watching paint dry or watching grass grow. If you want excitement, take $800, and go to Las Vegas.

—Paul Samuelson

Stock, also known as shares or equity, symbolizes a slice of ownership in a company. It grants you a claim on dividends and, hopefully, a share in the company's financial success through appreciation. To harness the growth of companies, savvy investors allocate a significant portion of their assets to stocks. Generally, there are two types of stock—common and preferred.

Common stock is your everyday stock. When folks chat about stocks, they're usually talking about these. Historically, common stocks have outperformed nearly all other investment types. But remember, with great potential returns comes great volatility. The market is like a roller coaster with its ups and downs, and to reap long-term benefits, you'll need to buckle in for the ride.

Preferred stock is like the quieter cousin. It mixes elements of bonds and stocks. Safer than common stocks but riskier than bonds, preferred stocks offer more stable dividends and sometimes, a shot at price appreciation. However, for simplicity's sake, we'll focus mainly on common stocks from here on out.

The stock market, on a long enough timeline, trends upward. Crafting the right strategy and sticking with it can significantly grow your wealth over time. Yes, markets have bad days, or even years, but these dips are typically followed by triumphant returns to new heights.

Stocks are traded on exchanges—places like the New York Stock Exchange (NYSE) or NASDAQ. These can be actual physical locations or virtual spaces where stocks are bought and sold. Equity investments are categorized in several ways—growth, value, large-cap, and more, spanning various sectors from technology to healthcare to, most recently, digital assets.

For the individual investor, there are three primary ways to invest in stocks:

1. **Individual stocks**: Buying shares in specific companies like Amazon or Apple.

2. **Mutual funds**: These pools of money are managed by professionals who invest in a diversified portfolio of stocks.

3. **Exchange-traded funds (ETFs)**: Similar to mutual funds but traded like individual stocks on an exchange.

Now, the million-dollar question: How should you invest in stocks? While individual stocks might seem glamorous, they require significant capital to diversify effectively. Mutual funds and ETFs offer a more practical route to diversification. They can track everything from the S&P 500 to specific industries or regions. ETFs and mutual funds come in two flavors: passive and active. Passive funds aim to mirror the returns of an index, while active funds strive to beat the market, often with higher costs.

Passive investing, especially through ETFs, tends to be more cost-effective and tax-efficient, making it an attractive option for many investors. ETFs are priced throughout the day and can be more flexible than mutual funds, which typically only price at the end of the trading day.

In conclusion, while you might hear tales of stock market glory, the steady and disciplined approach of investing in broad, diversified ETFs often leads to the best long-term results. Forget the high-stakes gambling of stock picking and enjoy the slower, more predictable path to wealth accumulation.

Have you ever been tempted to chase the high returns of a hot stock, only to regret it later? What's your understanding of the importance of diversification in your portfolio? Remember, investing isn't about excitement—it's about making strategic choices that grow your wealth reliably over time.

22

The Name
Is Bond

An investment in knowledge pays the best interest.

—Benjamin Franklin

Bonds: the unsung heroes of the financial world, often overshadowed by their flashier cousin, stocks. While stocks are like owning a piece of a company, bonds are more about lending your money to an entity, be it a corporation or government, in exchange for regular interest payments.

A fixed-rate bond is akin to a reliable old car: it pays you consistent interest semiannually until it reaches its maturity date. Unless the issuer defaults, you can predict your returns quite accurately if you hold the bond until it matures.

Now, let's talk about the main thrill (or risk, depending on your perspective) with fixed-rate bonds: interest rates. When rates go up, bond prices typically go down, and vice versa. This inverse dance is tied to a concept called "duration," which measures a bond's sensitivity to rate changes. For instance, if you're holding a bond from the Barclays US Aggregate Bond Index, which has a duration of about 5.98 years, a 1% rise in interest rates could decrease your bond's value by roughly 5.98%.

Longer-term bonds usually offer higher interest rates because you're taking on more risk, especially with rates potentially fluctuating. They're also rated for safety—the safer the bond, the lower the yield. It's the classic risk-reward trade-off.

If you've got a hunch that interest rates are going to drop, bonds might be your best friend. Locking in a high rate now means more value later if rates fall. But if rates rise, your bond's payout might look measly compared to new, higher-yielding options, and its market value could drop.

Venturing into bonds for higher yields without understanding the risks can be like jaywalking with your eyes closed. Unlike the near-zero risk of savings accounts or money market funds, fixed-rate bonds juggle the tricky interest-rate risk.

Bonds, whether through individual purchases, mutual funds, or ETFs, deserve a spot in balanced portfolios, especially as you edge closer to retirement. A mix of different maturities can help manage risks associated with changing interest rates.

As retirement approaches, ramping up your bond allocation can smooth out the bumps of a volatile market. Remember, as your horizon shortens, so should the duration of your bonds to align with your decreasing risk tolerance.

Now, are you clear on how bond values inversely relate to interest rates? Do you see how incorporating bonds could add a layer of stability to your investment portfolio? Consider adjusting your bond exposure as you transition into retirement, mixing in shorter-term bonds to safeguard your nest egg.

23

A Crash Course on Retirement Accounts

My interest is in the future
because I am going to spend the rest of my life there.

—Charles Kettering

Let's dive into the riveting world of retirement accounts, a topic slightly less exciting than watching paint dry but monumentally more rewarding for your future self.

Defined Benefit Plans: Also known as pensions, these are like the dinosaurs of the retirement world: impressive, but mostly extinct in the corporate realm. If you're sporting one from a governmental job, kudos! You have a set income waiting at retirement based on your salary and years of service. But watch out—some of these funds are as well-funded as a teenager's piggy bank.

Defined Contribution Plans: These are the modern workhorses of retirement savings. Think 401(k)s for the corporate warriors and

403(b)s for the non-profit knights and public sector sages. You put in your cash, and sometimes your employer chips in too, which is like getting a small lottery win. The beauty? You decide how much to contribute, usually through a pain-free payroll deduction.

Employers often match contributions up to a certain percentage, making it possible to boost your retirement savings without lifting a finger—well, other than to sign up. There's often a vesting schedule tied to these matches, meaning you earn the right to keep them over time, much like leveling up in a video game.

In 2024, you can stash away up to $23,000 in these plans. Choose between pre-tax contributions, which give you a tax break today, or after-tax contributions that let you withdraw tax-free at retirement—a choice between delayed or instant gratification, tax-wise.

Self-Employed Plans: For the solo flyers out there, options abound. SEP-IRAs, Solo 401(k)s (including a Roth option), and SIMPLE IRAs let you save with flexibility and, often, generous limits. It's like having your cake and eating it too, provided you're disciplined enough to bake the cake in the first place.

IRAs for Everyone:

- **Traditional IRAs** let you deduct contributions now and pay taxes later. The max you can contribute in 2024 is $7,000, or $8,000 if you're over 50—like getting a senior discount before you're a senior.

- **Roth IRAs** are the cool kids on the block: you pay taxes now but get tax-free money when you retire, which is pretty sweet if you expect to be in a higher tax bracket later.

- **Spousal IRAs** are for the stay-at-home partner, ensuring everyone gets a slice of the retirement pie, whether working or not.

This brief primer on retirement accounts barely scratches the surface. With rules changing as often as fashion trends, staying informed is crucial. But the core idea remains the same: whether it's pre-tax or after-tax, putting money aside today means you can kick back and relax tomorrow without worrying about your finances.

So, are you making the most of your retirement savings options? Could you be saving more? Are you ready to commit now for a comfortable retirement later? Remember, every little bit you save today is a gift to your future self. Make it count!

24

Unraveling Annuities

Truth is ever to be found in simplicity,
and not in the multiplicity and confusion of things.

—Isaac Newton

Annuities are the craps tables of the financial world—intimidating at first glance with myriad options that can bewilder even the savviest investors. Just like craps, where sticking to simple bets like Pass or Don't Pass gives you decent odds, understanding the basic types of annuities can cut through their complex facade.

What Exactly is an Annuity? An annuity is a contract with an insurance company. You give them cash either in a lump sum or through payments, and they promise to pay you back with interest, either right away or in the future. It's supposed to provide a steady income during retirement, which sounds great until you get into the nitty-gritty.

Phase One: Accumulation This is when you're paying into the annuity. Depending on whether your annuity is fixed or variable, your payments are invested differently. Fixed annuities offer a stable interest rate, kind of like a supercharged savings account. Variable annuities, on the other hand, let you choose from a menu of investments (like mutual funds), and your returns will vary based on how these investments perform.

Phase Two: Payout This is the good part—when you start getting money back. You can choose to get payments for life, for a set number of years, or some combination of both. If you choose wisely, you can have a nice, predictable income stream. If not, well... let's just say it's important to choose wisely.

The Catch: Fees and More Fees Annuities are notorious for their fees. There are surrender charges if you withdraw your money early, mortality and expense fees (which are as grim as they sound), and fees for managing the investments in variable annuities. All these fees eat into your potential returns. And if anyone tries to tell you that annuities are cost-free, remember—they're probably getting a nice commission for selling you one.

Are They Ever a Good Idea? In theory, yes. Annuities can provide a stable income, which is great for retirement. But because of their high costs and complex terms, they're often better in theory than in practice. If the financial industry starts simplifying and lowering costs for annuities, they might become a more attractive option. Until then, they're a bit like that overpriced, flashy casino game that promises big payouts but often delivers disappointment.

So, What's the Takeaway? Before you jump into an annuity, think of it like a high-stakes game at the casino. Know the rules, understand the odds, and be aware of all the fees. And maybe, just maybe, consider simpler, more transparent investment options first.

Are you holding an annuity and feeling a bit lost? It might be time to take a closer look and decide if it's really the best home for your money. Remember, sometimes the best bet is walking away from the table.

25

Smoke and Mirrors

The truth is what works.

—William James

Ever been invited to a steak dinner with the promise of a financial strategy "too good to refuse"? Enter the stage, the equity-indexed annuity (EIA)—an investment option that's been served up by insurance agents, garnished with impressive-sounding promises that you can cash in on market upswings without ever feeling the sting of a downturn. Sounds delicious, right? Well, the truth might give you indigestion.

Steak and EIAs: A Costly Pairing One fine evening, tempted by the prospect of a free steak, I found myself among the audience of one such seminar. Despite the "limited seating" warning, there seemed to be plenty of room for one more. The presentation was slick, the returns promised were dizzying—an alleged average of 8% annually, risk-free. By dessert, the room was buzzing with excitement. I, however, left early—the steak was the only good part of my evening.

The Gritty Details Equity-indexed annuities are complex beasts. They are marketed as straightforward investments but unpacking their layers reveals a labyrinth of terms and conditions. They might eke out gains that barely outpace inflation, but once you account for the hefty fees—often hidden deep within the contract—those gains might dwindle to less than the seasoning on your dinner steak.

The Real Cost of 'Free' And oh, the commissions! Up to 10% might go directly to the charming person who convinced you to sign up, all from your pocket. Accessibility to your own money comes with strings attached too. Want more than 10% of your funds in a year? That'll cost you, thanks to exorbitant surrender charges that can stretch over two decades.

A Tower Built on Fees Ever noticed how insurance companies often inhabit the tallest buildings in town? There's a reason they can afford such real estate, and products like EIAs contribute to this. It's troubling to think even well-meaning agents might be as caught up in the spin as their clients, believing they're doing good amidst a sea of red flags.

Regulation: A Slow-Moving Beast Despite tighter regulations around financial products, EIAs have slipped through the nets, largely thanks to a robust insurance lobby. While there's talk of clamping down on excessive fees and ensuring transparency, the EIA remains a glaring example of what's still wrong with the industry.

The Takeaway If you're pondering an equity-indexed annuity, or if you've already RSVP'd to that steak dinner, think again. You might find the cost of the meal is far higher than the price of a steak at your local butcher. As for EIAs, they're a gamble where the house—and the insurance companies—almost always win. Cook your steak at home and invest your money in products where the terms are clear, and the returns are straightforward. Your future self will thank you.

26

Avoiding Bad Bets

One does not accumulate but eliminate.
It is not daily increase but daily decrease.
The height of cultivation always runs to simplicity.

—Bruce Lee

Imagine stepping into a casino for the first time: lights flashing, slot machines singing, and every game imaginable beckoning. It's easy to get caught up in the glitz, but if you're smart, you'll play it cool and stick to the games with the best odds.

In the lineup of not-so-great choices, blackjack insurance, craps prop bets, keno, and slot machines take the cake for the worst bets. They're designed to pull you in and drain your wallet. And don't get me started on lotteries—they're essentially a tax on hope, especially taxing for those who dream big but earn small.

Now, I have a soft spot for poker. It's the only game in the casino where you're not up against the house but fellow players—some of whom have more dollars than sense. If you're eyeing poker, start small with friendly games, and avoid diving into high-stakes waters without a sturdy life vest of experience. Trust me, you don't want to learn the hard way by becoming fish food at my table.

Navigating your financial future is a bit like walking through that casino. There are plenty of flashy options that promise big payouts but usually end up costing you more in the long run. Avoid these as if your wallet depends on it—because it does.

Making wise investment choices requires dodging the bad bets. It's like avoiding the wrong life partner—choose poorly, and you'll regret it for a long time. Switching jobs for what seems like a dream position can also backfire. Not every shiny opportunity is gold; some are just glitter-covered traps.

As you venture through the financial casino, remember: the house always has the edge, and in the world of investments, that house is often not on your side. Learn to spot the bad bets, sidestep the traps, and your journey toward financial simplicity and success will be all the smoother. Caveat emptor—let the buyer beware indeed.

"Keep it simple, stupid." This pithy advice from the US Navy perfectly captures the essence of smart investing. Overcomplicating things can be your downfall. Here's a quick rundown of the investment blunders you'd be wise to steer clear of—yes, even those seemingly bright folks (me included) have fallen for these:

- **Paying High Fees:** Just like overpaying for a cup of coffee, it's unnecessary.

- **Unrealistic Expectations:** Hope is not a strategy. Keep your financial feet on the ground.

- **Failing to Diversify:** Putting all your eggs in one basket? A rookie mistake.

- **Ignoring Pre-Tax Investments:** We'll circle back to this but think of it as leaving free money on the table.

- **Falling in Love with a Stock:** This isn't a rom-com. Don't get attached.

- **Chasing Performance:** That's like driving by looking in the rearview mirror. Spoiler: You might crash.

- **Taking Too Much or Too Little Risk:** Balance is key. Know your financial self.

- **Day Trading:** Most day traders lose money—don't join the club.

- **Trading Options, Futures, and Commodities:** Leave these high-stakes games to the pros.

- **Buying "Hot Tips" from Uncle Louie:** Family BBQs are for burgers, not stock tips.

- **Buying on Margin:** Borrowing money to invest? That's a slippery slope.

- **Chasing Yield:** High returns come with high risks. If it sounds too good to be true, it probably is.

- **Buying Illiquid Financial Products:** Flexibility in finance is a must. Keep it fluid.

- **Buying Promissory Notes:** If offered, kindly decline and consider calling the authorities.

- **Ignoring Inflation:** It's the silent killer of buying power.

- **Investing in Depreciating Assets:** Always aim for assets that appreciate. Investing 101.

The world of personal finance doesn't have to be a labyrinth. Embracing simplicity in your investment strategy not only makes life easier but also aligns more closely with achieving your financial goals. Avoid these bad bets like outdated fashion trends—they're not coming back in style.

Got a history of betting on the wrong horse? It's time to change the game. Are you ready to simplify your financial life and commit to smarter, straightforward investing? Remember, investing should be about making your future self a lot richer, not giving you grey hairs

27

Look Before You Leap

Nothing is more disgusting than the majority:
because it consists of a few powerful predecessors,
of rogues who adapt themselves,
of weak who assimilate themselves,
and the masses who imitate
without knowing at all what they want.

—Johann Wolfgang von Goethe

Homeownership is often touted as a smarter financial move than renting, hailed as a key pillar of the American Dream. People argue that renting is akin to tossing your money into a bonfire. True, owning a home means it's yours (well, yours and the bank's), shields you from the fickleness of landlords, and offers potential tax breaks and equity growth. The chorus sings loud and clear: Buy a house and watch your wealth grow!

But let's tap the brakes for a reality check. The 2007 housing crash taught a hard lesson: the belief that real estate prices only go up is as shaky as a house of cards in a windstorm. Those who thought they were sitting pretty in ever-appreciating homes learned otherwise when the bubble burst. Remember, hindsight is always 20/20. Could those fortune-building years return? Maybe. As of March 2024, home prices look inflated, with the Case Shiller Index suggesting homes are significantly overvalued compared to historical norms. Buying now? Could be dicey.

Then there's the beloved mortgage interest deduction. Once a persuasive argument for buying, recent tax reforms have zapped much of its value. The Tax Cuts and Jobs Act of 2017 nearly doubled the standard deduction, making the mortgage interest deduction irrelevant for many. And property taxes? They're still deductible, but when you do the math, the fiscal magic might not be as spellbinding as it once was.

Ownership isn't just about signing papers; it's about ongoing maintenance, the possibility of sudden moves due to life changes, and the costs that come with both. Renters, by contrast, enjoy a flexibility that homeowners might envy when life throws a curveball.

So, should you cross homeownership off your list? Not necessarily. It's a serious long-term commitment that should be weighed carefully against other financial priorities like boosting retirement savings or building an emergency fund. And what about using extra cash for buying income-generating properties? It's tempting, especially if you've heard tales like my poker buddy who flipped his way to a fortune—before crashing back to reality without an exit strategy.

Before you leap into buying, consider the full picture. Homeownership isn't just an investment; it's a lifestyle choice with profound financial implications. Are you ready for that? Could renting or buying something smaller free up resources to build wealth in other ways?

Here are some questions to mull over:

- Have you really crunched the numbers on what owning a home costs, including those evaporating tax benefits?

- Are you prepared to delay homeownership to hit other financial milestones?

- Can you think of homeownership as a luxury rather than a mere investment?

Sometimes, less is more. Opting for a humbler abode or continuing to rent might just be your ticket to financial flexibility and growth

28

In the Unlikely Event

Everybody has a plan until they get punched in the mouth.

—Mike Tyson

It's an apt metaphor for life's unexpected turns, especially when it comes to the world of insurance. While it's crucial to have a safety net, diving headfirst into the sea of insurance products without a clear understanding is like trying to swim with weights. You need just enough insurance to float comfortably—not so much that you sink under the weight of unnecessary premiums. Let's navigate through the maze of various insurance types.

Life Insurance: It's pretty straightforward—life insurance ensures that your family won't face financial hardships if you pass unexpectedly. Think of it as replacing your economic value to your loved ones. We'll dive deeper into which policies make sense and how to calculate the necessary coverage later.

Disability Insurance: These policies are your income's bodyguard if you're unable to work due to disability. Many get this through work, but it's also available independently. Short-term disability might be overkill if you're a good saver, but long-term disability insurance is worth considering, especially if saving isn't your forte.

Health Insurance: This one's a moving target, thanks to ever-changing political winds. If you're not covered through work, hunting through the marketplace is a must. At the very least, secure catastrophic coverage to guard against financial ruin from major medical bills. And yes, the cost of healthcare is a topic hotter than a Carolina Reaper pepper—spicy and painful but impossible to ignore.

Long-Term Care Insurance: Flip a coin—heads, you might need long-term care as you age; tails, you might not. These policies cover expenses like nursing homes or home care that Medicare won't. They're pricey, so if you're building a significant nest egg, you might self-insure through your savings instead.

Property and Casualty Insurance: Drive a car? You need auto insurance. Own a home? You need homeowner's insurance. These are no-brainers because they're often legally required. But even if the law doesn't require it, protecting your assets is a smart play. Opting for higher deductibles can lower premiums if you have an emergency fund to cover those deductibles if and when they are needed.

Renters Insurance: Renting doesn't mean you can skip insurance. Renters insurance is a bargain in most cases and covers everything from your gadgets to your garb. Plus, it kicks in even if you're traveling and something happens to your belongings.

Umbrella Liability Insurance: This is the cloak of invisibility for your assets, extending beyond the coverage limits of your standard policies. It's relatively cheap for the coverage it provides, which makes it a no-brainer for protecting yourself against major claims that could otherwise dry up your financial reservoir.

In summary, before you leap into any insurance commitments, take stock of what you truly need. Are you over-insured, under-insured, or just right? Regularly reviewing your policies and comparing the market can save you a bundle and keep you appropriately covered. Remember, more insurance isn't always better—sometimes, it's just more.

29

Financing Higher Education

Education is what remains
after you have forgotten everything you learned in school.

—Anonymous

With tuition rates skyrocketing significantly faster than inflation and wages, the burden of student loans has reached an all-time high of $1.77 trillion in 2023, surpassing even credit card debt and second only to mortgages.

Opinions vary on who should bear the cost of a college education. Some parents feel it's their duty to foot the bill, while others believe this financial responsibility should fall to the students themselves. Regardless of where you stand, there are proactive strategies to help lessen this financial load.

Scholarships and Grants:

If your offspring are high achievers or excel in sports, they may be eligible for grants and scholarships—this is the closest thing to free money you'll find in the education sector. Platforms like Scholly offer a cost-free service (as of 2024) matching students with potential scholarships. Moreover, taking Advanced Placement (AP) courses can reduce the number of required college classes, potentially shortening the degree completion time and saving money. Also, consider the stark cost differences between in-state and out-of-state tuition, which could influence your decision on where they should apply.

Saving Strategies:

For parents inclined to support their children's educational pursuits financially, starting early is key. While Coverdell Education Savings Accounts (ESAs) allow for flexible investment choices, they're limited by a modest annual contribution cap of $2,000 and are fading in popularity.

Custodial Accounts:

These allow you to save for your child's future, but with a catch: the money legally belongs to your child once they reach adulthood. This could impact their eligibility for need-based financial aid and doesn't guarantee the funds will be used for education.

529 Plans: The Optimal Choice:

A more robust option is the 529 savings plan, which offers significant tax advantages. Contributions are made on an after-tax basis and can grow tax-free if used for qualified educational expenses. In 2024, you can contribute up to $18,000 annually ($36,000 for married couples filing jointly) without triggering gift taxes. You can also front-load five years' worth of contributions up to $90,000 under the same tax-free umbrella. An added benefit is that the account holder can change the beneficiary, providing flexibility if plans change.

This strategy not only allows for substantial tax savings but also keeps the control of funds in the hands of parents, which can be crucial for managing how the funds are ultimately used. This financial tool provides a practical pathway to managing the rising costs of higher education, ensuring you're investing wisely in your child's future without compromising your financial health.

With a 529 plan, flexibility is your friend. If your firstborn decides college isn't in their cards—perhaps they prefer a motorcycle journey to academia—you can easily transfer the plan's benefits to another family member. And remember, you're not married to your state's 529 plan. Shop around for any state's plan that offers the best mix of investment choices and tax advantages.

Roth IRAs: Dual-Purpose Power Tool

If your income fits within the limits, a Roth IRA isn't just for retirement. As of 2024, single parents earning under $146,000, or $230,000 for those married and filing jointly, can contribute up to $7,000 annually (or $8,000 if you're 50 or older). Funds drawn from a Roth IRA come out as contributions first (thanks to FIFO accounting), which means they're tax-free and penalty-free.

Let's say you stash away $7,000 annually in a Roth for 15 years. Your nest egg blossoms to $250,000, split between $105,000 in contributions and $145,000 in gains. That $105,000? It's all yours to use, tax-free, whenever you need it. The remaining gains continue to grow and are safeguarded for your future retirement.

Student Loans as a Backstop

Despite your best saving efforts, if the college fund isn't quite where it needs to be, federal student loans offer a viable plan B. Subsidized loans don't accrue interest until your progeny caps off their collegiate career, providing a financial breather. Unsubsidized loans accumulate interest immediately, but they're there if you need them.

Early Birds Get the Degrees

The sooner you begin saving, the more you benefit from compound interest—time is indeed your best ally in growing college funds. Remember, various savings tools each offer unique benefits, and your approach can be tailored to fit your financial situation and educational goals.

Are you ready to take responsibility for your child's educational future? Have you started funneling funds towards this goal? Remember, laying the groundwork now will make all the difference later. Start today and keep your future options open and flexible.

30

Budget Is Not a Four-Letter Word

A budget tells us what we can't afford,
but it doesn't keep us from buying it.

—William Feather

Many poker aces have tumbled from high rollers to broke rollers, not from lack of skill, but from ignoring a golden rule: Never bet more than you can afford. They ignored their financial limits, hoping bravado could replace planning. It couldn't.

Let's face it: About 40% of Americans steer clear of budgets, according to CNBC in 2023. A year later, Yahoo Finance highlighted that nearly a quarter of American households spent more than they earned. These figures aren't just numbers; they're a financial cry for help.

Here's the straight deal: Most Americans are spending beyond their means, tumbling deeper into the debt pit every month. Sounds gloomy, right? It doesn't have to be. With a bit of discipline and a solid budget, you can escape this cycle.

Yes, the dreaded "B" word—budget. It might make you cringe, but without it, your financial goals are as good as dust. Think of a budget not as a chain but as a blueprint that helps you build a stable financial future. It forces you to confront the real state of your finances—no rose-colored glasses allowed.

A well-planned budget helps you distinguish between 'wants' and 'needs.' Ask yourself before every purchase: Do I need this, or do I just want it? Is that trendy gadget or chic outfit worth delaying your financial goals?

Getting Started Is Half Done

How do you start? Track every dollar for a month. Go old school with a pen and notebook, or tech it up with apps like Mint. Prepare to be shocked at how those little purchases add up—yes, even that daily artisan coffee.

Here's a personal tidbit: One of my daughters, fresh out of college, was baffled by how she blew through her paycheck despite minimal expenses. A deep dive into her spending habits revealed a $1,500 monthly splurge on non-essentials like fancy dinners and impulse buys. She didn't really need another blouse, but who was keeping track?

Tracking her spending was a game-changer. She tightened the reins, swapped dining out for home-cooked meals, and guess what? She started saving. It turns out, budgeting didn't mean the end of fun—it just painted fun in a different color.

You Don't Have to Cut Corners, Just Paint Better Lines

Embracing a budget doesn't mean you have to live like a hermit. It's about prioritizing financial security over fleeting pleasures. Maybe you discover your inner chef instead of eating out. Maybe you realize that the car can last another year, and the house doesn't need an upgrade just because your salary got a bump.

Remember, each small decision can have a long-term impact on your financial health. Those daily lattes, lottery tickets, or the latest tech gadget? Each purchase should be a conscious decision, not a reflex.

If the thought of budgeting sends your stomach into knots, you're not alone. But trust me, once you start, what felt like financial shackles will soon feel like financial empowerment. It's amazing how much easier life gets when you're not constantly worried about money.

So, are you ready to give budgeting a shot? Can you transform this new habit into your financial backbone? It's not just about saving money—it's about saving your future financial self.

If you've never budgeted before, now's as good a time as any to start. After all, managing your money wisely isn't just about avoiding debt; it's about creating a future where you're in control. Dive into budgeting and watch your savings—and your peace of mind—grow.

31

The FUEL

There is no dignity quite so impressive,
and no independence quite so important, as living within your means.

—Calvin Coolidge

Imagine a poker table where some players throw in their rent money, hoping luck will be more loyal than logic. Predictably, these players often leave with lighter pockets. It's a classic example of what not to do—gamble with scared money. Similarly, managing personal finances without a cushion for the unexpected is like playing poker without seeing your cards. It's a bad bet.

Surprisingly, the magic solution to financial woes isn't discovering the next Apple or Google, nor is it found in a lucky break. It's actually quite mundane but effective—spend less than you earn. This leftover, my friends, is what I like to call the FUEL.

Debt often creeps up from living beyond our means, and trust me, it's a formidable barrier to wealth accumulation. People sometimes seem more comfortable confessing to extramarital affairs than revealing their credit card balances. It's that taboo. But embracing a shift in how you view debt can transform your financial health and self-esteem.

Strategies to Fight Debt:

1. **Cut the Credit:** Start by putting those credit cards on ice—literally, if you must. Use them only for necessities and pay off the balance monthly to avoid interest charges.

2. **Budget for Debt Reduction:** Make room in your budget to pay more than the minimum payments. Prioritize debts with the highest interest rates.

3. **Windfalls as Debt Wipeouts:** Use unexpected money, like tax refunds, to make significant dents in your debt.

And here's a thought: if you can't afford it, don't buy it. Revolutionary, right? This simple advice could save countless people from debt despair.

The 50:30:20 Rule for Financial Clarity:

- **50% on Essentials:** Half of your after-tax income should cover absolute necessities like housing and groceries.

- **30% on Wants:** Yes, you can still have fun—just keep it to 30%.

- **20% is your FUEL:** This is for paying down debts, saving for emergencies, and investing. Why 20%? It's that sweet spot that could allow you to retire on a nest egg worth 25 times your annual income, assuming conservative growth and income projections.

Consider the story of a young college graduate who balked at putting 15% of his $40,000 salary into his company's retirement plan. He claimed it was unaffordable. A month prior, he'd been mowing lawns for pocket change. Perspective is everything. He thought a plush bed and a big-screen TV were essentials, overlooking the opportunity to begin growing his wealth substantially.

Remember, living on 80% of your income isn't just possible; it's liberating. Start by saving something—anything. As you adjust, gradually increase your savings rate. Before you know it, saving becomes second nature.

Do you currently follow the 50:30:20 Rule, or are you a financial thrill-seeker, betting more than you can afford to lose? Can you envision yourself adopting a structured budget to streamline your financial life?

Embrace the challenge to live within 80% of your income. It's not just about avoiding financial ruin; it's about securing financial independence. Let's make the commitment to fuel our futures, not our fears.

32

You Should
Be Committed

Until one is committed, there is hesitancy,
the chance to draw back, always ineffectiveness.

—William Hutchison Murray

Achieving financial freedom isn't just about having the cash; it's about making a steadfast commitment and sticking to your plan until you see results. It's easy to talk a big game about financial goals, but without that ironclad dedication, plans are just pretty words that never take flight.

Commitment is your secret weapon. It's what transforms dreams into reality. This journey is less about your financial acumen and more about your readiness to do whatever it takes. You have to start with a clear assessment of where you are, arm yourself with the necessary knowledge, and then dive headfirst into the execution phase—no excuses, no backing down.

Consider my friend, the late-blooming marathon runner. Starting in her forties, she set a lofty goal: run a marathon in every state and then on every continent. Now, she's more than halfway there.

Her secret? She just started running—one block at a time, until one block turned into miles. She told me, "Once you can run five miles, scaling up to 26.2 miles is just a matter of extending your commitment a bit further each time."

Her story is a powerful metaphor for financial planning. Like training for a marathon, securing your financial future is about persistence and incremental progress. It's about making a plan, starting small—perhaps with saving a little from each paycheck—and gradually increasing your efforts as your financial stamina improves.

Are you the type who starts a project with enthusiasm but fizzles out before the finish line? Do you find yourself overwhelmed by the scope of achieving financial freedom? Has the dream of financial independence seemed just out of reach?

Now is the perfect time to make a commitment. A real, no-escape, no-excuse commitment to becoming financially free. Remember, "Well begun is half done." Start simple, stay focused, and keep pushing forward. Every small step you take is a piece of the foundation you're building for a secure financial future.

Are you ready to lace up your financial running shoes and start the race to financial freedom? Why not start today, and see just how far your dedication can take you?

33

The Missing Link

I have been impressed with the urgency of doing.
Knowledge is not enough; we must apply.
Being willing is not enough; we must do.

—Leonardo da Vinci

It's like poker—reading every book won't turn you into a champion until you've actually sat at a table, chips stacked, facing opponents with every intention to claim your stash. The real test comes when the dealer starts dealing. The same holds true for the financial strategies you've read about here. The theories are solid, sure to bear fruit, but the question is: will you plant the seeds?

Consider health: everyone knows eating well and exercising are good for you, much like managing your finances responsibly is crucial for wealth. Yet, knowing isn't enough. We don't benefit from vegetables we haven't eaten or from money wisdom we haven't practiced. What often goes missing is the crucial bridge between knowing and doing, a gap wider than it appears.

Consider the business world, where companies understand the need for change but get stuck in perpetual planning or endless consulting without actual implementation. That paralysis by analysis? It's real, and it's a growth killer.

I keep a sign in my office that reads: "Those who talk should do, and only those who do should talk." It's a daily reminder that actions speak louder than meetings.

Fear is a major blocker. Fear of failure, of the unknown, can keep you from even trying. But here's the thing: a life without risks is like a book without conflict—dull and uninspiring. Failures? They're just lessons in disguise, often teaching us more than success ever could.

Many of my clients, overwhelmed by the magnitude of planning for retirement, divert to safer conversations—like their next golf trip to Pinehurst. Don't be that person. Ignoring your financial health is like skipping physical check-ups; it only leads to worse complications.

So, what's your fear? Start small if you must. Baby steps are still steps. Want to run a marathon? Start with a jog around the block. Dream of playing guitar? Pick one up and strum your first chord. Need to lose weight? Swap out that slice of cake for a crisp apple.

Knowledge is just potential power. It gains real power when acted upon. If you're aiming for a retirement where you control your time and finances, the steps are clear in the execution section that follows. It's time to act, not just ponder.

So, ask yourself:

- Are you a great planner but a poor doer?

- Does thinking about the future send shivers down your spine?

- Can you commit to starting now, however small the step may seem?

It's time to transform knowledge into action. Let's stop talking about financial freedom and start making it happen.

34

Knowledge Recap

Give me six hours to chop down a tree,
and I will spend the first four sharpening the axe.

—Abraham Lincoln

We've navigated the investment landscape together, separating the sound strategies from the dubious ones. Here's a brief recap to keep your investment toolkit sharp and effective:

- **Recognize Who's Who:** Understand the credentials and motives behind the menagerie of reputed financial advisors.

- **Ignore the Noise:** Don't let the daily media frenzy sway your investment decisions.

- **Assess the Rake:** Understand the impact of fees on your investments and ensure you're getting value for money.

- **Vet Your Advisor:** If you choose to work with an investment advisor, don't be shy—ask probing questions.

- **Simplify Your Stocks**: Stick to passive ETFs for stock investments.

- **Choose Safe Bonds**: Prefer passive ETFs for bond holdings as well.

- **Understand Your Retirement Options**: Know the retirement plans available to you and master their details.

- **Just Say No to Annuities**: Consider other more transparent and less costly investment options.

- **Skip the Sales Pitch**: Avoid high-pressure sales dinners and too-good-to-be-true offers.

- **Avoid Gambling on Investments**: Steer clear of high-risk financial moves and bad bets.

- **Rethink Homeownership**: Weigh the benefits and downsides critically, stepping away from conventional wisdom.

- **Sort Out Insurance**: Prepare for the unexpected by choosing the right insurance.

- **Save Smart for Education**: Start early and explore every avenue like scholarships and 529 plans to ease tuition costs.

- **Budget Religiously**: Manage your money with a clear and realistic budget.

- **FUEL Your Future**: Allocate resources wisely to power your investments.

- **Commit Wholeheartedly**: Dedicate yourself fully to your financial plan.

- **Act on Your Knowledge**: Don't just accumulate information—apply it.

Let's keep it simple: limit your investments to those that are cost-effective and have a proven track record of success. With your financial "axe" well-sharpened, you're ready to cut through the noise and make your mark.

EXECUTION

35

Follow
the Recipe

Numbers don't lie. Women lie, men lie, but numbers don't.

—Max Holloway

Picture Las Vegas, not just for its dazzling lights but for its world-class dining that can whisk you from an American steakhouse to a Parisian bistro in a single block. I indulge in this culinary paradise on every visit. Though I've been complimented on my cooking, don't expect to see me on a cooking show narrating the virtues of the perfect herb mix anytime soon.

Now, what's a cooking novice's best tool in the kitchen? A recipe. (Yes, this is a finance book, but bear with me!) Recipes are like treasure maps: they guide us to recreate dishes that seasoned chefs have mastered and refined. I've come to know my way around terms like "sauté" and "braise," and whether it's through a cookbook or a quick online search, I can start with a promising recipe, gather the needed ingredients, and dive in. It's as straightforward as baking a cake.

However, many have all the ingredients—the information and tools for financial success—at their fingertips yet never turn on the stove.

If that's been you, it's time for a change. What follows isn't just advice; it's a clear recipe for managing your finances effectively. To succeed, you can't just read; you must act. You might need to familiarize yourself with some new terms and adopt some healthier habits, but trust me, the rewards are worth it. You owe it to yourself and your loved ones to manage your money wisely. And remember, the first attempt at a cake might be daunting, but by the second or third, you'll wonder why you ever hesitated.

So, are you ready to learn? If so, preheat your oven—metaphorically speaking—and let's start crafting that flawless financial plan. Being open to guidance, even when it feels a bit uncomfortable, is the key to achieving not just financial stability but many of your life's goals.

36

The End Game

What you get by achieving your goals is not as important as what you become by achieving your goals.

—Zig Ziglar

Imagine you're at the helm of your financial ship, plotting a course for the golden years. Let's zoom in on Harold and Maude Stevens, a fictional couple who at thirty-five are trying to pin down their retirement strategy.

First things first: "When do you picture yourselves bidding adieu to the 9-to-5 grind?" I ask them.

"In thirty years, right at sixty-five," they reply in unison, like they've rehearsed it.

"Perfect! Now, how much would you need monthly to live comfortably if you retired today?" After a quick exchange of looks, Maude ventures, "Maybe $4,000?"

Alright, let's break it down. Annualize that monthly dream (4,000 x 12) to $48,000. To avoid the risk of outliving their savings, a 4% safe withdrawal rate is the gold standard. So, how much do they need in the kitty to kick back comfortably? Simple math: $48,000 x 25 equals a cool $1.2 million.

But wait, there's a twist—don't forget about inflation. Today's dollar will be tomorrow's spare change. Assuming an inflation rate of 3%, we need to adjust that $1.2 million. Fast forward three decades, and you're looking at needing close to $3 million to maintain the same purchasing power.

So, the goal for the Stevens? Stack up $3 million by the time they hit sixty-five to start drawing down a monthly inflation-adjusted $4,000. And that's just their starting point.

Table 1 – Harold and Maude Stevens Nest Egg Calculation

Number of years until retirement	30
Monthly income desired if they retire tomorrow ($)	4 000
Multiply by 12 to get	x 12
Annual income desired if they retire tomorrow ($)	48 000
Multiply by 25 to get	x 25
Nest egg required if they retire tomorrow ($)	1 200 000
Adjust the nest egg required tomorrow by an inflation rate of 3% to get the nest egg they will require in 30 years ($)	2 912 715

If this feels like algebra class all over again, take a deep breath. Grab a calculator, or better yet, punch those figures into my favorite on-line helper at www.thecalculatorsite.com. Bookmark it; it's a gem for future number crunching.

And don't just spectate—run your numbers too. What does your Point B look like? Calculate what you need to save to ensure your retirement isn't just timely but timeless.

Table 2 - Your Nest Egg Calculation

Number of years until retirement	
Monthly income desired if you retire tomorrow ($)	
Multiply by 12 to get	x 12
Annual income desired if you retire tomorrow ($)	
Multiply by 25 to get	x 25
Nest egg required if you retire tomorrow ($)	
Adjust the nest egg required tomorrow by an inflation rate of 3% to get the nest egg they will require in 30 years ($)	

Though the mountain of $3 million might seem steep, remember: it's all about starting somewhere and sticking to it. Can you follow this recipe? Are these calculations sparking ideas, or do they just spark confusion?

Commit to understanding and navigating your path to financial freedom. Your Point B is waiting—how will you get there?

37

Ready, Set, Go: Financial Planning Basics

The best time to plant a tree was twenty years ago.
The second-best time is now.

—Chinese Proverb

If you're gearing up to sprint towards financial security, knowing where you stand right now—your Point A—is crucial. This is where we dive into the nitty-gritty of your current financial health by calculating your net worth, which is simply all that you own minus all that you owe.

Let's take Harold and Maude Stevens as examples. They've calculated their assets (things they own) at $459,000 and their liabilities (things they owe) at $259,000. Subtracting the liabilities from the assets, they find themselves with a net worth of $200,000.

Table 3 – Harold and Maude Stevens Net Worth Statement

Assets	$	Liabilities	$
Home	350 000	Mortgage	250 000
Autos	20 000	Auto Loans	6 000
Emergency Savings	9 000	Credit Cards	3 000
Investments	50 000		
Personal Belongings	30 000		
Total	**459 000**		**259 000**
Net Worth (Assets – Liabilities)	200 000		

Now it's your turn. List down everything you own that can be converted into cash—think your home, car, investments, and that dusty collection of vintage comic books. Now tally up all your debts—the mortgage, car payments, that credit card bill that snuck up on you last Christmas. Subtract your total liabilities from your total assets, and voilà, you've got your Point A.

Table 4 – Your Net Worth Statement

Assets	$	Liabilities	$
Total			
Net Worth (Assets – Liabilities)			

But wait, there's more. Let's also factor in your income because, let's face it, money coming in is just as crucial as money going out. If you're flying solo, just add up your own income. If you're part of a dynamic duo like Harold and Maude, combine your earnings to get a complete picture.

Armed with your net worth and income, you're now ready to race from Point A to Point B, your financial freedom finish line. In the next chapter, we'll map out the course.

Have you scribbled down your assets and liabilities yet? Are you itching to figure out how you can bridge the gap from where you are to where you want to be? Knowing how to calculate your net worth is like having a financial compass—it'll always tell you where you are and help guide you to where you need to go.

38

Balancing Your Financial Diet: The 50:30:20 Rule

What gets measured gets managed.

—Peter Drucker, recipient of the Presidential Medal of Freedom

Let's dive into the financial life of Harold and Maude Stevens once again. Quick recap:

- **Point A (Starting Net Worth):** $200,000
- **Point B (Goal Net Worth):** $3,000,000
- **Time Horizon:** 30 years
- **Current Annual After-Tax Income:** $90,000

Remember the 50:30:20 Rule we discussed earlier? It's time to see how Harold and Maude stack up against this budgeting strategy.

Table 5 – Harold and Maude Stevens 50:30:20

	Yearly ($)	Monthly ($)
Gross Income	120 000	10 000
Net Income	90 000	7 500
Essentials Like Housing and Food (50%)	45 000	3 750
Discretionary Spending (30%)	27 000	2 250
FUEL (20%)	18 000	1 500

How the 50:30:20 Rule Breaks Down:

- **50% on Needs:** $45,000 (essential expenditures)
- **30% on Wants:** $27,000 (fun money)
- **20% on Savings or Debt Repayment (FUEL):** $18,000

Now, let's turn the spotlight on you. It's your turn to put this budget rule into action. Review your expenses from the past year—or at least the last few months. How does your financial diet measure up? If you're allocating 20% or more to FUEL, you're on track. If not, it's time to tweak your spending to ensure you're fueling your financial goals adequately.

Table 6 – Your 50:30:20

	Yearly ($)	Monthly ($)
Gross Income		
Net Income		
Essentials Like Housing and Food (50%)		
Discretionary Spending (30%)		
FUEL (20%)		

Running a household is akin to managing a small business: there's income, there are expenses, and ideally, there's profit (savings). Early in my budgeting adventures, I drowned in a sea of categories. While enlightening, it was also overkill. Now, I prefer a straight-forward approach—simply categorize expenses as essential or discretionary and ensure there's enough left for FUEL.

Even if budgeting feels foreign, the process is simple and can revolutionize your financial health. Don't let it turn into an obsession, though. Creating a scarcity mindset where you always fear never having enough can actually derail your financial progress. Instead, focus on understanding where your money goes to better control your financial future. Who knows? Maybe there's an unexpected windfall in your future.

In the next chapter, we'll explore how to power up with your FUEL.

Questions to Ponder:

- Are your essential and discretionary spending in check?
- Have you been successful in consistently saving?
- Is your FUEL tank frequently running on empty?

Implement the 50:30:20 Rule not just as a budgeting tool, but as a lifestyle choice that ensures you're always driving towards financial security. Let's make sure you're not just spinning your wheels but actually gaining traction on the road to financial freedom.

39

Rationing Your FUEL

Life is not a matter of holding good cards,
but sometimes, playing a poor hand well.

—Jack London

By now, you've identified your FUEL and are ready to distribute it effectively to carve a path to financial stability. Let's look at Harold and Maude Stevens as our model again. They've squirreled away a net worth of $200,000, which includes a manageable debt of $9,000, an emergency fund of $9,000, and investments totaling $50,000.

Harold and Maude have committed $18,000 annually to their FUEL, breaking down to $1,500 monthly. But how should this be sliced and diced?

First Bucket: Debt Reduction. Allocate 50% of your FUEL here. For Harold and Maude, that's $750 each month aimed at annihilating their debt. They'll pay off their higher interest credit card debt first while maintaining minimum payments on the lower-interest auto loan. The goal? Eliminate the most toxic debt quickly.

Second Bucket: Emergency Savings Fund. This should house at least three months of your after-tax income, prepared for life's unpredictable turns. For Harold and Maude, we're talking about a cozy cushion of $22,500. They'll allocate 25% of their FUEL—$375 monthly—until they hit this mark. Store this fund in a liquid, easily accessible account like a high-yield savings or money market account.

Third Bucket: Investments. The final 25% of their FUEL goes here. Prioritize any available employer-matched retirement plans first—after all, it's free money. Once Harold and Maude have extinguished their debt and padded their emergency fund, all their FUEL will shift towards maximizing these investments.

Table 7 - Harold and Maude Stevens Bucket Strategy

	Debt ($)	Emergency Savings ($)	Investments ($)
Point A ($)	9 000	9 000	50 000
Year 1 Allocation (%)	50	25	25
Year 1 Allocation ($)	9 000	4 500	4 500
Year 1 Balance ($)	0	13 500	54 500
Year 2 Allocation (%)	NA	50	50
Year 2 Allocation ($)	NA	9 000	9 000
Year 2 Balance ($)	0	22 500	63 500
Year 3 Allocation (%)	NA	NA	100
Year 3 Allocation ($)	NA	NA	18 000
Year 3 Balance ($)	0	22 500	81 500

Now, Your Turn. Using the Stevens' method as your template, calculate your own allocations. Here's what to do:

1. **Tally your assets and liabilities** to pinpoint your net worth.

2. **Determine your after-tax income** to set your budget baseline.

3. **Assign your FUEL** according to your most pressing financial needs.

Table 8 – Your Bucket Strategy

	Debt ($)	Emergency Savings ($)	Investments ($)
Point A ($)			
Year 1 Allocation (%)			
Year 1 Allocation ($)			
Year 1 Balance ($)			
Year 2 Allocation (%)			
Year 2 Allocation ($)			
Year 2 Balance ($)			
Year 3 Allocation (%)			
Year 3 Allocation ($)			
Year 3 Balance ($)			

As Harold and Maude journey from debt to a fully-funded emergency stash and grow their investments, follow their blueprint. Start with the most urgent financial needs and advance to long-term growth and security. By the end of the second year, with their debts settled and emergency fund secured, all of Harold and Maude's FUEL powers their investments.

Time to Check:

- Have you outlined a plan to allocate your FUEL?

- Are you prepared to adjust your budget to meet these goals?

- Can you commit to turning your financial planning into action?

This simple yet strategic approach to managing your FUEL will ensure you're not just spinning your wheels but actually driving towards your financial goals. Get ready, set your allocations, and watch your financial health improve!

40

Navigating Your Financial Journey

Our goals can only be reached through the vehicle of a plan,
in which we must fervently believe, a
nd upon which we must vigorously act.

—Pablo Picasso

A financial plan is your road map from your current financial situation (Point A) to your ultimate financial goal (Point B). This plan isn't just a nice idea—it's a must-have, and it needs to be concrete, with written goals, specific milestones, and enough flexibility to adapt to life's unexpected twists.

Let's revisit our friends, Harold and Maude Stevens:

- **Point A:** $200,000 net worth

- **Point B:** $3,000,000 target net worth

- **Time Horizon:** 30 years
- **Current Annual After–Tax Income:** $90,000
- **Annual FUEL:** $18,000 (20% of after-tax income)

Can Harold and Maude realistically turn their $200,000 into $3 million in 30 years? Absolutely—and here's the breakdown:

We'll adjust their FUEL for inflation at 3% per year and aim for an investment growth rate of 6% annually. While the idea of "assuming" might make us uneasy, a 6% return is conservative enough to keep our estimates realistic.

Using a compound interest calculator, I crunched these numbers:

- Harold and Maude start with a net worth of $200,000 and $18,000 in FUEL.
- They increase this by 3% each year.
- Their investments grow at 6% annually.

Lo and behold, at the end of 30 years, their calculations show a net worth of approximately $3.2 million—surpassing their goal!

Now, your turn:

1. Plug in your own Point A as the initial balance.
2. Set the growth rate at 6%.
3. Input your financial horizon.
4. Choose yearly compounding.
5. Add your annual FUEL, adjusted for 3% inflation.
6. Hit calculate.

If your timeline is shorter, or your starting point is less, you'll need to adjust either by increasing your FUEL contributions or setting a more modest Point B. Remember, financial planning is not about perfection; it's about progression.

And what if life throws you a financial windfall—a bonus, a tax refund, or an inheritance? Before you splurge, think about boosting your FUEL. Increasing your contributions can significantly shorten the time needed to reach Point B or even expand what Point B could look like.

Use these calculations for other goals too—whether it's saving for a dream vacation, a second home, or your children's education. Yes, enjoy life's pleasures now and again, but remember, the most substantial rewards come from consistent, disciplined saving.

Keep on reading to discover smart investment strategies to make your financial dreams a reality. Have you mastered the compound interest calculator yet? What insights have you gained? Are you seeing your financial plan take shape? Visualize your journey from Point A to Point B, and let's make those dreams tangible.

Questions to ponder:

- Have you become comfortable with the compound interest calculator?

- What has surprised you in your financial calculations?

- Is your financial blueprint ready to guide you to your goals?

41

Playing the Game

Seek, above all, for a game worth playing.
Such is the advice of the oracle to modern man.
Having found the game, play it with intensity—play as if your life
and sanity depended on it. (They do depend on it.)
Follow the example of the French existentialists and flourish a banner
bearing the word "engagement." Though nothing means anything,
and all roads are marked "NO EXIT," yet move as if your movements
had some purpose. If life does not seem to offer a game worth playing,
then invent one. For it must be clear, even to the most clouded
intelligence, that any game is better than no game.

—Robert S. de Ropp, from *The Master Game*

Investment strategies, like poker games, don't come with guaranteed wins, and anyone promising a foolproof plan is probably selling you something you don't need—or they've had a little too much of their own Kool-Aid. My realization about how closely poker strategies paralleled investment behaviors didn't strike me in a boardroom but rather, oddly enough, at a poker table.

Poker and investing both demand a cold patience and a resilience against emotional play. It's the tortoise's game in a world that celebrates hares. You're already learning one of the optimal plays by engaging with this book.

Consider poker: it's less about the cards and more about reading the room. In Las Vegas, I used to probe my tablemates about their origins—tourists playing for thrills versus locals playing for bills. The tourists typically played with abandon, treating their chips like disposable income, while the locals employed a meticulous strategy, often collecting steady, small wins.

Shortly after selling my business in 2012, I took my cues from these Vegas regulars and tried my hand at professional poker. I played long, hard hours, treating the game like a job. It paid off financially, but sitting in a dimly lit casino day after day wasn't for me. I learned that while the money was good, sunshine and a less sedentary lifestyle were better.

That stint fine-tuned my investment philosophy. I used to be what you'd call a market timer, buzzing from the adrenaline of potentially high returns. But, like a reformed gambler, I stepped back from the high-stakes game to appreciate the steady reliability of a buy-and-hold strategy.

The thrill seekers in the stock market might dart from stock to stock, but it's the steady, unemotional investors who tend to see the most consistent growth. If you're looking for a lesson in patience, remember that even in the chaos of a casino, there's wisdom in playing a slow, steady hand.

Now, as market fluctuations come and go, I aim to stay as composed as a seasoned blackjack player counting the deck. Boredom, I've learned, has its dividends.

So, let's lay our cards on the table:

1. If you've got a crystal ball, maybe it's time to auction it off—after all, who knows what it's really worth?

2. Can you turn a deaf ear to the next hot tip from Uncle Louie?

3. Are you ready to check your ego and embrace a more measured approach to investing?

It's about time in the market, not timing the market. Let's play the long game.

42

Selecting Your Financial Playground

*Don't gamble; take all your savings and buy some good stock
and hold it till it goes up, then sell it. If it don't go up, don't buy it.*

—Will Rogers

Imagine investment as a buffet. You've got your retirement accounts front and center, demanding your attention first—here's where to pile your plate. You can contribute to these accounts before or after taxes are taken out, each with its merits. Diversify between the two to hedge your bets, allowing you to pick the tax advantage that suits your palate best when retirement rolls around.

Here's why this buffet strategy is wise:

- **Pre-tax contributions** reduce your taxable income now, meaning you pay less tax and have more money growing. For instance, shelling out $1,000 pre-tax only feels like $700, assuming you're in the 30% tax bracket.

- **Tax-deferred growth** means your investments grow undisturbed by taxes, which can significantly accelerate your wealth building.

- **Automated contributions** make investing as habitual as your morning coffee. Direct deposits from your paycheck streamline the process, subtly adjusting your spending habits.

- **Early withdrawal penalties**—while seemingly harsh—act like a stern guardian of your funds, discouraging dipping into your savings prematurely.

When it comes to the type of retirement accounts, the menu is vast: 401(k)s, 403(b)s, traditional IRAs, Roth IRAs, and more. If your job offers a 401(k) with matching funds, jump on that first—it's essentially free money.

After maxing out these accounts, then consider the à la carte options like nonqualified investment accounts, which are like ordering off the menu: no special tax treatments (apart from potential long-term capital gains) but still delicious.

Leaving a job? You'll face three choices with your retirement plan:

1. **Cash out** and face taxes plus penalties—like eating a whole cake in one sitting.

2. **Stay put** with limited investment options and possibly higher fees.

3. **Roll over** into an IRA, broadening your investment choices and potentially reducing costs.

Choose wisely. If the choice isn't clear, re-read the options like the fine print on a dinner menu.

Avoid putting all your eggs in one basket. Uncle Louie's stock tips might be tempting, but a well-diversified portfolio is your best bet. Think about your timeline: the longer it is, the spicier you can go with risk. Regular investments harness the power of dollar-cost averaging, helping you buy more when prices are low and less when they're high, all without emotional decisions influencing your strategy.

So, before you invest:

- Are you fully utilizing any employer-matched retirement contributions?

- How much can you invest pre-tax to lower your current tax bill?

- Focus your investment FUEL primarily on these tax-advantaged accounts to supercharge your financial growth.

Let's get investing, and remember, it's not about getting rich quick but cultivating wealth over time.

43

Crafting Your Investment Strategy

People do not wish to appear foolish; to avoid
the appearance of foolishness, they are willing to remain actually fools.

—Alice Walker

Navigating the investment landscape can feel like trying to choose a dessert at a buffet without knowing the calorie count. The elusive concept here? Risk. Let's demystify this with a blend of humor and hardcore facts.

Many folks think of risk as the Big Bad Wolf of investing. It's not so scary once you understand it. There are tools out there to measure your risk tolerance—essentially, how much investment fluctuation can you stomach without losing sleep? If you're loaded with cash, you might flirt with risk like it's a dark and mysterious stranger. But if your pockets aren't as deep, you might treat risk like that cousin you avoid at family reunions.

Here's the kicker: feelings shouldn't drive your investment decisions. Got twenty years before you need your cash? Maybe you should stop eyeing the "safer" bets and embrace a bit of volatility. Remember, the longer the runway, the bigger the plane you can land—or in investment terms, the more risk you can handle.

For simplicity, I advocate for three investment portfolio types, cheekily named to help you remember:

- **Far Better Aggressive**: For the young guns, with more than a twenty-year time horizon.

- **Far Better Moderate**: For those mid-range planners, with a ten- to twenty-year time horizon.

- **Far Better Conservative**: For the nearly-there crowd, with a two- to ten-year time horizon.

If you're looking to spend your money in less than two years, stick it in a money market fund where it's as safe as cookies in a locked jar.

Let's break down the Aggressive portfolio: think 90% stocks, 10% spicy alternatives. As you age, or your needs draw nearer, you introduce bonds to calm the party down, shifting eventually to a Conservative mix—60% stocks, 30% bonds, and 10% spicy alternatives.

Heads up on fees—they nibble away at your returns like termites on wood. I lean towards ETFs (exchange-traded funds) because they're like buying the whole grocery store instead of picking individual ingredients. They're cheap (think expense ratios as low as 0.03%), diversified, and you can trade them without burning a hole in your wallet.

When setting up your portfolio, start with ten equally-weighted positions. Easy enough. Maintain a close balance by simply adding future investments where your percentage allocations are the lowest at that juncture—forgoing the need to sell any holdings unnecessarily or prematurely. This is called being tax savvy.

So, as you ponder your investment strategy, ask yourself:

- Are my investments a well-blended smoothie of diversified assets?
- Does my portfolio's spice level match my time horizon?
- Am I overpaying for the pleasure of investing?
- Am I ready to slash those pesky fees and keep more cash in my pocket?

Set up your ETF portfolio to mirror your risk appetite and timeline, and you're all set. This way, you're not just playing the investment game; you're strategizing to win.

44

Constructing Diverse Portfolios

I think that the first thing is that you should have a strategic asset allocation mix that assumes that you don't know what the future is going to hold.

—Ray Dalio

Embarking on the investment journey without a map can be as daunting as it is risky. That's where strategic asset allocation comes into play. Let's imagine your investment plan is a global buffet—featuring a smorgasbord of U.S. equities, international delights, the steady staple of bonds, and a sprinkle of alternatives like Bitcoin. Each of these categories/sectors should be portioned according to how much volatility (or culinary adventure) you can stomach, which we fondly call your "risk profile."

Table 9 – Far Better Portfolio – Master

	Aggressive Allocation (%)	Moderate Allocation (%)	Conservative Allocation (%)
US Equity	60	50	50
Non–US Equity	30	20	10
Fixed Income	0	20	30
Alternative	10	10	10
Total	100	100	100

Once you've decided your appetite for risk, it's time to pick the ingredients. And by ingredients, I mean exchange-traded funds (ETFs). These nifty little packets of investment joy are detailed in Tables 10 through 12. Whether you're shopping at Fidelity or Schwab, these ETFs are as accessible as your local grocery store—assuming your local grocery store stocks a diverse array of global investment options.

In a nutshell, opting for diversified, low-cost (less than 0.1%), and tax-advantaged portfolios isn't just smart—it's investing with a safety net. And who wouldn't want that when venturing into the great unknown of future markets?

Table 10 – Far Better Portfolio – Aggressive

US EQUITY	ETF	Ticker	%
Large-Cap Blend	Schwab US Large-Cap	SCHX	10
Large-Cap Growth	Invesco QQQ	QQQ	10
Mid-Cap Blend	Schwab US Mid-Cap	SCHM	10
Small-Cap Blend	Schwab US Small-Cap	SCHA	10
Small-Cap Value	Vanguard Small-Cap Value Index	VBR	10
Real Estate	Schwab US REIT	SCHH	10
Non-US Equity			
Foreign Large-Cap Blend	Schwab International Equity	SCHF	10
Foreign Large-Cap Value	iShares Core MSCI Total International Stock	IXUS	10
Emerging Markets	Schwab Emerging Markets Equity	SCHE	10
Alternative			
Bitcoin	Fidelity Wise Origin Bitcoin	FBTC	10

Table 11 – Far Better Portfolio – Moderate

US Equity	ETF	Ticker	%
Large-Cap Blend	Schwab US Large-Cap	SCHX	10
Large-Cap Growth	Invesco QQQ	QQQ	10
Mid-Cap Blend	Schwab US Mid-Cap	SCHM	10
Small-Cap Blend	Schwab US Small-Cap	SCHA	10
Real Estate	Schwab US REIT	SCHH	10
Non-US Equity			
Foreign Large-Cap Blend	Schwab International Equity	SCHF	10
Foreign Large-Cap Value	iShares Core MSCI Total International Stock	IXUS	10
Fixed Income			
Intermediate-Term Government Bond	Schwab Intermediate-Term US Treasury	SCHR	10
Long-Term Government Bond	Vanguard Long-Term Treasury Index	VGLT	10
Alternative			
Bitcoin	Fidelity Wise Origin Bitcoin	FBTC	10

Table 12 - Far Better Portfolio - Conservative

US Equity	ETF	Ticker	%
Large-Cap Blend	Schwab US Large-Cap	SCHX	10
Large-Cap Growth	Invesco QQQ	QQQ	10
Mid-Cap Blend	Schwab US Mid-Cap	SCHM	10
Small-Cap Blend	Schwab US Small-Cap	SCHA	10
Real Estate	Schwab US REIT	SCHH	10
Non-US Equity			
Foreign Large-Cap Blend	Schwab International Equity	SCHF	10
Fixed Income			
Intermediate-Term Government Bond	Schwab Intermediate-Term US Treasury	SCHR	10
Long-Term Government Bond	Vanguard Long-Term Treasury Index	VGLT	10
Intermediate-Term Corporate Bond	Vanguard Intermediate-Term Corporate Bond Index	VCIT	10
Alternative			
Bitcoin	Fidelity Wise Origin Bitcoin	FBTC	10

45

You Can Be a DIY Investor

The role of the musician is to go from concept to full execution.
Put another way, it's to go from understanding the content of something
to really learning to communicate it
and make sure it's well-received and lives in somebody else.

—Yo-Yo Ma

Imagine walking into a swanky poker den not as a gambler, but as the house. Intriguing, right? Hosting such a game (strictly hypothetically, as it skirts the edge of legality) could teach you a lot about managing risks and rewards—much like managing your own investments. Just as the house siphons a small cut from every pot, a DIY investor smartly manages their fees to maximize returns.

Now, not everyone is cut out for the DIY route. Just like some would rather pay for a gourmet meal than fumble through a complex recipe. If you've decided to manage your own investments, this book is your recipe book, and I'm here to help you cook up some financial success without the Michelin-star chef fees.

Let's dive into the financial lives of our friends, Harold and Maude Stevens. Say they've been paying a 1% management fee on their investments, which grow at a net annual rate of 6%. If they ditch the advisor, keep that 1% for themselves, and notch up their returns to 7%, their retirement pot could swell significantly—think in the tune of an extra $740,725. Not too shabby for a little extra legwork!

However, there are times when the cost of an advisor is justified. Tax planning, for example, can be a labyrinth that might require a professional's map. But for the everyday management of stocks and bonds? There's a slew of technology that can help. Enter robo-advisors—like Betterment or Schwab's Intelligent Portfolios—that offer to manage your investments for a fraction of the cost of human advisors.

Robo-advisors strip out the emotion—often the investor's worst enemy—and they're perfect for anyone who feels a bit queasy at the thought of flying solo right out of the gate. If Harold and Maude used a robo-advisor charging only 0.5% in fees, they could see their fortune further inflate to around $3.5 million, proving sometimes the middle road is the most lucrative.

So, if the idea of going full DIY on your investments scares the wallet out of your pocket, consider starting small. Manage a portion of your portfolio yourself and see how it feels. Like dipping your toes into the ocean, it might be chilly at first, but pretty soon, you'll be ready to dive in headfirst.

Have you dared to manage your own investments yet? Does the thought make you more nervous than a long-tailed cat in a room full of rocking chairs? Are you ready to try handling just a slice of your portfolio to start? Take control, step by step. You might just find it's not as daunting as it seems.

46

Cover
Your Ass

We have two lives,
and the second one begins we realize we only have one.

—Confucius

Here's a humorous truth: Consulting a life insurance agent about whether you need more insurance is akin to asking a chocolatier if you should try more truffles. They're selling comfort in the guise of prudence.

Let's cut through the jargon. Life insurance is essentially about not leaving your loved ones financially adrift. Striking the right balance—where you're not hemorrhaging cash on unnecessary premiums yet not skimping on necessary coverage—can feel like trying to thread a needle while riding a roller coaster.

Think of your estate as a mix of assets you own (your life estate) and the benefits you pass on upon death (your death estate). When you're young, the bulk of your estate is essentially what your life insurance policy can payout because, let's face it, you're just starting to accumulate wealth. Over time, as your assets grow, they begin to offset the need for insurance. Eventually, your life estate might grow big enough to serve as your entire estate.

So, what's the real deal with life insurance? It's about replacing income lost with the untimely demise of the breadwinner. It's not about insuring your kids because—harsh truth alert—they're economic drains, not assets. As much as you love your little angels, insuring them doesn't financially benefit your estate.

How much coverage do you need? The old-school wisdom suggests a tidy formula: aim for about twenty-five times the annual income you'd want to replace. Why this figure? Because withdrawing 4% annually from this amount is considered a safe bet for ensuring the money lasts a lifetime. For instance, if you're pulling in $60,000 a year, a $1.5 million policy should do the trick. That way, your beneficiaries could theoretically pull $60,000 yearly without ever running dry, assuming smart investments.

Now, which life insurance to buy? If you're eyeing coverage worth twenty-five times your income, whole life or universal life policies might make you wince at the price tag. They're often prohibitively expensive. Instead, consider term life insurance. It's straightforward: if you kick the bucket during the term, your beneficiaries get the payout. No frills, no cash value accumulation, just pure and simple coverage. Choose a term that lines up with your retirement plans or when your youngest kid graduates from college. You get a fixed premium and a fixed payout, keeping things predictable.

Remember, the goal here isn't to turn into an insurance shopping fanatic but to smartly cover your bases so you can sleep soundly at night. And maybe, just maybe, save that extra cash for a family vacation or two.

Are you feeling better about navigating the insurance maze? Ready to balance coverage with cost effectively? Have you checked your current policies lately? Time to button up your financial safety net without overpaying for peace of mind.

Here's a grim, yet amusing truth: Statistically, the sooner you shuffle off this mortal coil, the longer your loved ones will need to finance their earthly endeavors. When contemplating life insurance, imagine the unthinkable—you're flattened by a rogue bus tomorrow. It's a morbid exercise, but vital. What financial legacy would you leave behind? Would your spouse need to sell the house? Could your kids still go to college without student loans stalking them post-graduation? And who's going to cover the sudden daycare costs?

Life insurance isn't just about you; it's a lifeline for those you leave behind. This isn't a popular dinner topic, for sure, but it's one that can save a lot of future headaches and heartaches. A thoughtful approach considers debt elimination, educational needs, and the adjustments to a household budget minus your income. Yes, it's a lot, but hey, nobody said adulting was going to be easy.

Now, here's a kicker that life insurance salespeople love to trot out: if you outlive your term life insurance, you've essentially paid for something you didn't use. So what? That's the point! It's like buying a parachute when flying; you don't buy it hoping to use it, you buy it just in case. Plus, let's face it, those guys aren't fond of selling term insurance because it pays them beans compared to whole or universal life policies. Remember, your job isn't to make sure your insurance agent can afford his sports car.

Consider our friends Harold and Maude Stevens. They're parents to a toddler and an infant, raking in a combined $120,000 annually. Crunching numbers the way only nerds like us love, they'd need a $1.5 million term policy each to cover life's ugly surprises, with a term that carries them until the youngest kiddo caps off college life. A twenty-year term might do, but why not price out thirty while you're at it? The cost difference can be surprisingly paltry.

Life insurance, your "death estate," should dovetail with your asset accumulation, your "life estate." It's there to fill the financial gaps while you build your empire. By the time Harold and Maude hit their mid-fifties, if they've played their cards right and avoided any buses, they'll be sitting pretty on a $3 million nest egg, ready to churn out a cushy $10,000 a month in retirement.

Table 13 – Harold and Maude Stevens Life and Death Estate

Age	Life Estate ($)	Death Estate ($)	Total ($)
35	200 000	1 500 000	1 700 000
40	378 474	1 500 000	1 878 474
45	634 966	1 500 000	2 134 966
50	998 672	1 500 000	2 498 672
55	1 509 166	1 500 000	3 009 166
60	2 219 707	0	2 219 707
65	3 202 520	0	3 202 520

Term life insurance isn't just a personal financial tool. It's a Swiss Army knife for the financially savvy, covering everything from family protection to business agreements. And let's not forget, if health issues make your premiums skyrocket, you might need to adjust the face value or term length to keep it affordable.

Do you have life insurance, or are you playing financial Russian roulette? Is your life insurance fit for purpose, or is it time for a tune-up? Think of life insurance as your fiscal parachute. It's better to have it and not need it than need it and not have it.

47

Providing for Your Loved Ones

A man has made at least a start on discovering
the meaning of human life when
he plants shade trees
under which he knows full well he will never sit.

—D. Elton Trueblood

Ben Franklin famously said the only certainties in life are death and taxes. But let's add another certainty: chaos. Yes, failing health or an unexpected accident might stop you from ruling your financial empire one day, but there's no dodging the final curtain call. So, why not ease the burden for your loved ones and organize your estate like you'd organize your sock drawer—meticulously and with great foresight?

I've slotted estate planning into the 'Execution' section for a reason. It's because this isn't something you can just think about doing—it's something you absolutely must do. Procrastination here isn't just unwise; it's potentially disastrous, leaving both financial messes and heartaches in its wake.

First things first: If you have kiddos or assets—or, heck, even a beloved pet goldfish—start with a will. This isn't a grim dinner party topic, but it's as necessary as knowing where the fire exit is in a crowded theater. A will dictates what happens when you're dancing at the great disco in the sky. If your situation is straightforward, an online will kit can do the job without breaking the bank. More complex estates might need the charm and expertise of a seasoned attorney.

Without a will, you leave the fate of your assets up to the cold, impersonal state laws. Now, who wants a stranger telling them where their hard-earned treasures should go?

Things to include in your will:

- **Executor/executrix:** This is your financial quarterback. Choose wisely, and make sure they're up for the game.

- **Beneficiaries and their shares:** Who gets what, whether it's your spouse, kids, or a charity dedicated to saving retired circus elephants.

- **Guardianship details:** Who's taking the reins if your kids are still running around in capes pretending to be superheroes?

- **Funeral specifics:** Maybe you want fireworks, or perhaps just a playlist with your favorite hits. Let 'em know.

Now, onto the power of attorney (POA). This gem lets someone you trust manage your affairs if you're out of commission. And don't forget about a durable power of attorney (DPOA), which keeps you covered even if you're permanently out of the office, so to speak.

A living will, or advance directive, isn't about your finances—it's about your final days. Make your medical wishes clear because, let's face it, you don't want your estranged cousin deciding whether to keep the life support running.

And let's talk about making things super easy for those you leave behind. Craft an emergency-records kit that contains all your critical info—legal documents, passwords, the secret family recipe for lasagna—everything your chosen one might need to know.

Finally, don't be a stranger to your own documents. Review them every few years or after major life events. Adjust as needed because life loves a good plot twist.

Are your affairs in order? Do you have a will that reflects your current wishes? Have you planned for the inevitable in a way that ensures minimal drama and maximum ease for your loved ones? Remember, the best legacy is one that's well planned.

48

One for You, Nineteen for Me

The general who wins the battle
makes many calculations in his temple before the battle is fought.
The general who loses makes but few calculations beforehand.

—Sun-Tzu

George Harrison's frustration while penning "Taxman" is something many of us can relate to after a glance at our own tax bills. Remember, the Beatles were being hammered by taxes to the tune of 95% at their peak—keeping a mere 5% of their earnings. That's less than what's left in a toddler's bowl after a spaghetti meal!

Let's face it, April 15th might as well be a national day of mourning in the United States. While the days of hiding money under the taxman's nose are long gone, there are still a few tricks in the book to keep your hard-earned money away from Uncle Sam's grasp, legally, of course.

The most recognized game in town for tax savings is the retirement plan—think traditional IRAs or 401(k)s. These beauties let you stash cash before the taxman sees it, reducing your taxable income and letting your investments grow tax-deferred. Say you're pulling in $60,000 annually and manage to squirrel away $6,000 into your 401(k); your taxable income magically drops to $54,000. Voila! Less tax today, more fun tomorrow.

But not all retirement accounts are created equal. Enter Roth IRAs and Roth 401(k)s, where you pay taxes on money going in, so you can skip paying them on the way out—including the gains. Perfect if you're betting you'll be in a higher tax bracket when you retire because who knows, right?

Here's a pro tip: Split your bets. Keep a foot in both traditional and Roth accounts. This way, when it's time to draw down, you can choose from which pot to take—depending on whether you're having a good or bad tax year. Think of it as tax-time Tetris.

And for those in the know, don't overlook the Health Savings Account (HSA). This little gem lets you put away money tax-free, and then spend it tax-free on qualified medical expenses. It's like a double coupon day every day for health expenses!

Now, if you're an investor outside the retirement account sphere, ETFs are your new best friends. Unlike mutual funds, which can hit you with unexpected taxable events, ETFs are sleek, efficient, and tax-friendly. They let you control when you take hits, allowing for strategic planning around capital gains taxes.

Finally, consider turning a hobby into a business. Love to travel? Start a blog, write off your trips, and maybe make a few bucks while you're at it. It's a win-win—you enjoy your travels, and the tax code works in your favor, not against you.

In the battle against taxes, the more you plan, the more you save. So, pull out your calculator and start strategizing like a general in the temple. After all, it's your money—shouldn't you keep as much of it as possible?

Now, ponder this:

- Are you maximizing the benefits of various retirement accounts?
- Could an HSA help you reduce your taxable income?
- What hobby could you monetize to reap tax benefits? Tax planning might not be fun but think of it as the financial equivalent of brushing your teeth: ignore it at your peril.

49

The Annual Review

*The discipline of writing something down
is the first step toward making it happen.*

—Lee Iacocca

Annual reviews aren't just for employees. To keep your financial life in prime condition, carve out time every year to sit down—yes, with actual paper and pen if you must—and review your finances. If you're part of a duo, make it a date night. Flying solo? An accountability partner can be your financial gym buddy.

The Stevens have done a solid job during their first five years.

Transparency in your financial life is like lifting weights in front of a mirror—you see exactly what needs work and what's already strong. And remember, being honest about money is more brave than brash.

Investment performance can be as unpredictable as a cat on a skateboard, but here's what you can control: sticking to your budget. If you've been faithful in feeding at least 20% of your after-tax income to your FUEL, then you're likely on the right track.

Table 14 – Harold and Maude Stevens Annual Review

Age	FUEL Budget ($)	Life Estate Budget ($)	Death Estate Budget ($)	Total Estate Budget ($)
36	18 000	230 580	1 500 000	1 730 580
37	18 540	275 552	1 500 000	1 775 552
38	19 096	299 076	1 500 000	1 799 076
39	19 669	337 323	1 500 000	1 837 323
40	20 259	422 722	1 500 000	1 922 722
	FUEL Actual ($)	Life Estate Actual ($)	Death Estate Actual ($)	Total Estate Actual ($)
36	18 000	242 803	1 500 000	1 742 803
37	15 000	266 054	1 500 000	1 766 054
38	20 000	303 006	1 500 000	1 803 006
39	25 000	328 890	1 500 000	1 828 890
40	24 000	404 166	1 500 000	1 904 166

To kick off your review, tackle these questions:

- Are the goals and timelines you set still clear in your mind?
- How closely did you stick to the 50:30:20 Rule in your budgeting?
- Is your debt taking a nosedive?

- Are your emergency funds looking more like a safety net and less like a tightrope?

- Did at least 20% of your after-tax income consistently go into FUEL?

- How did your investments perform over the past year?

- Are your investments still a good match for your risk tolerance?

- Have you managed to keep your cool and make rational financial decisions?

- Were your investments as tax-efficient as possible?

- Is your life insurance coverage still fitting your needs?

- What financial habits are you proud to have adopted?

- Which bad financial habits have you kicked to the curb?

- What tweaks can you make to improve next year?

- Have you considered starting a side hustle for extra income?

- Most crucially, are you actually doing what you planned to do?

Don't just think it—ink it. Record your actual figures against your forecasts to measure your progress. Need help with the math? Again, www.thecalculatorsite.com is your go-to for running those numbers.

Remember, perfection is not the goal; progress is. You might find it helpful to check in more frequently—quarterly reviews can help keep you on track without feeling overwhelmed at the year's end.

What additional metrics could help sharpen your financial review? Are you ready to embrace this level of scrutiny? Why write it down? Because what gets written gets done.

Gear up, dive deep, and let this annual review pave the way to a more secure financial future.

50

The Myth of Multitasking

A master in the art of living draws no sharp distinction between his work and his play; his labor and his leisure; his mind and his body; his education and his recreation. He hardly knows which is which. He simply pursues his vision of excellence through whatever he is doing, and leaves others to determine whether he is working or playing. To himself, he always appears to be doing both.

—Lawrence Pearsall Jacks

In the modern world, where the ping of a smartphone can yank us from deep thought to cat videos in a heartbeat, being truly present is akin to pulling off a magic trick. While technology has turned us into wizards of productivity, it's also made us champions of distraction.

From the endless scroll of fake news to the posture-wrecking allure of smartphones—giving chiropractors everywhere a reason to cheer—technology serves up a feast of contradictions. I can video call halfway across the globe for free, yet I shudder at the 24/7 availability it demands. My parents thought of me as a tech guru, while my kids laugh at my struggles with the latest apps. And don't get me started on the irony of my addiction-prone brain getting lost in Netflix binges or the black holes of Google searches.

Here's a nugget of truth to chew on: multitasking is a myth. The human brain is wired for focus, not juggling. Trying to do several things at once doesn't boost productivity—it just muddles it. Think of the mind like a mischievous monkey, hopping from branch to branch, never sitting still. This "monkey mind" can sabotage everything from professional goals to personal hobbies.

In my youth, a golf club had my undivided attention, and I played pretty well. These days? Not so much. My mind's clutter has taken a serious toll on my swing. The remedy I've found? Meditation. Taking time each day to quiet the monkey mind helps me regain clarity and calm.

Poker, interestingly enough, demands my full attention—it's like meditation, where each play clears away the mental clutter, much like solving a jigsaw puzzle during a rainstorm. If only my golf game could use avail itself of that kind of focus!

In today's flexible work environment, where home offices are the new norm and 9-to-5 is going the way of the dodo, maintaining a balance between professional and personal life is trickier than ever. How do we manage this new reality? Can we draw a line in the sand when our teenager treats the dinner table like a phone booth?

Reflect on these points:

- How often do you really disconnect from the digital world?
- Does technology serve you, or have you become its servant?
- When was the last time you did absolutely nothing, and just enjoyed the moment?

Embrace the challenge of being present. Forget multitasking and cultivate the art of single-tasking—doing one thing at a time, fully and well. It's not just about improving productivity; it's about enhancing the quality of your life, one focused moment at a time.

51

Execution Recap

The difference between what we do
and what we are capable of doing
would suffice to solve most of the world's problems.

—Mahatma Gandhi

You've now got a toolbox that should, in theory, take you from 'here' to 'financial nirvana'. My mission was to strip down the complex beast of personal finance management so that anyone—even those who still use flip phones—can master it. But (and it's a big but), you've got to be the one to swing the hammer. Here's the essence of execution, distilled into actionable steps:

1. **Be Coachable:** Embrace the guidelines laid out here like a sous chef follows a recipe from Gordon Ramsay—meticulously and with a bit of fear.

2. **Define Your Goals:** Envision your financial endgame with clarity. Keep that vision in your crosshairs always.

3. **Assess Your Now:** Take a hard look at where you stand financially today—warts and all.

4. **Embrace Budgeting:** Adopt the 50:30:20 Rule not just as a guideline but as a lifestyle.

5. **Allocate Your FUEL:** Strategically use your resources to extinguish debt, bolster your emergency fund, and invest wisely.

6. **Plan Your Journey:** Craft a detailed roadmap from Point A (today) to Point B (retirement dreams).

7. **Invest Intelligently:** Focus on tax-efficient strategies and understand where and how to invest.

8. **Choose Smart Investments:** Opt for passive ETFs tailored to your timeline.

9. **DIY Investing:** Step (slowly if necessary) into the role of managing your own investments and keep what you would have paid in fees.

10. **Secure Life Insurance:** Buy term insurance to protect your loved ones without breaking the bank.

11. **Sort Your Estate:** Don't procrastinate on estate planning—it's about as optional as breathing.

12. **Tax Planning:** Become a tax-savvy investor and keep more of your hard-earned money.

13. **Annual Reviews:** Like a pilot reviewing flight instruments, check your financial trajectory regularly.

14. **Stay Present:** Cultivate mindfulness. The art of being present enhances decision-making and reduces mistakes.

It's on you to turn these strategies into actions. Remember, this isn't just about accumulating wealth; it's about creating a life that feels rich in all the right ways. So, crank up your resolve, chart your course, and maybe—just maybe—you'll find that making it happen is more rewarding than dreaming about it.

52

Waxing Philosophical

What is not started today is never finished tomorrow.

—Johann Wolfgang von Goethe

Ever since my Vegas debut in the sweltering summer of '78, the poker table has been more than a battleground of wits—it's been my window into the human dance with dollars. Some players cash in, many fold, yet the house always gets its cut.

Why the relentless gaming against staggering odds? Why do so many skip the rulebook before risking their paycheck? Why does every card sharp believe they're the sharpest? It mirrors the bigger gamble: personal finance. Why do so few retire well-heeled in a land ripe with opportunity? Why buy into ventures that are Greek to them? Why does money flow like water for some but stick like glue to others? These ponderings spurred me to pen this book.

I'm a veteran of the school of hard knocks, with enough missteps to fill volumes. Procrastination delayed this book's birth by longer than I care to admit. Despite knowing better early on, I didn't practice what I preached. But that's old news now, and like me, you're here to bridge the infamous gap between knowing and doing.

Ironically, despite a career in finance, money itself doesn't stir my soul. It's a necessity, yes—a facilitator of transactions. My daughter, a gifted musician, wishes time away, craving a life lived solely in the now. I empathize with her disdain for the necessary evil that is currency. I've seen firsthand how money's dark side can corrupt.

Yet, I've also witnessed the remarkable good it can achieve. I needed to reconcile the need for wealth without letting it rule me. Gradually, I reframed my relationship with money, treating it like the strategic game it is, and mastering it became a fulfilling endeavor. Writing this book is the cherry on top.

In my neighborhood poker game, a twenty-dollar win is a cause for celebration. My mom often bested me in gin rummy, with victories rarely exceeding a dollar, yet the bragging rights were priceless. To me, the joy of the game transcends the cash involved.

In the arenas of poker and finance, it's no longer about the money; it's about playing the game well. That shift in perspective has made all the difference. No matter your past financial faux pas, it's never too late for a turnaround. You've got the tools now—compound interest (the world's eighth wonder) and solid strategies from these pages.

Start simple, keep your eyes on the prize, and enjoy the journey.

Shuffle up and deal.

If you can keep your head when all about you
Are losing theirs and blaming it on you;
If you can trust yourself when all men doubt you,
But make allowance for their doubting too:
If you can wait and not be tired by waiting,
Or, being lied about, don't deal in lies,
Or being hated don't give way to hating,
And yet don't look too good, nor talk too wise;
If you can dream— and not make dreams your master;
If you can think— and not make thoughts your aim,
If you can meet with Triumph and Disaster
And treat those two impostors just the same;
If you can bear to hear the truth you've spoken
Twisted by knaves to make a trap for fools,
Or watch the things you gave your life to, broken,
And stoop and build 'em up with worn-out tools;
If you can make one heap of all your winnings
And risk it on one turn of pitch-and-toss,
And lose, and start again at your beginnings,
And never breathe a word about your loss:
If you can force your heart and nerve and sinew
To serve your turn long after they are gone,
And so hold on when there is nothing in you

Except the Will which says to them: "Hold on!"
If you can talk with crowds and keep your virtue,
Or walk with Kings—nor lose the common touch,
If neither foes nor loving friends can hurt you,
If all men count with you, but none too much:
If you can fill the unforgiving minute
With sixty seconds' worth of distance run,
Yours is the Earth and everything that's in it,
And— which is more— you'll be a Man, my son!

From "If" by Rudyard Kipling

Acknowledgments

Crafting this book has been a wild ride—exhilarating and daunting in equal measure. I couldn't have navigated it without a horde of extraordinary people.

First off, a heartfelt nod to my late mom, Catherine Currie. No string of words can fully capture how profoundly you've shaped me. Your unwavering faith in me, against all odds, was my linchpin. I feel your presence deeply every day.

A huge thanks to my editors, Janet Wagner and Jesse Winter, who were more than just grammatical gatekeepers—they were my cheerleaders, convinced that my ramblings needed a global audience. Your patience and gentle nudges transformed me from a scribbler into a raconteur.

Doug Dalton, the poker maestro of Bellagio, thank you for swinging open the doors to the high-stakes sanctum and rooting for my project from the get-go.

To Lyle Berman—tycoon, poker legend, and repository of the best tales from the felt—your time and tales were golden. You got what I was trying to do, and you got behind it.

Remembering Chip Reese, a titan of the poker world, who generously schooled a neophyte like me. Your legacy at the table is unmatched. Rest well.

A shout-out to Tim Ferris, whose wisdom reshaped my approach to life and work—you turned on the lights.

To my local poker crew—Farley, Deano, Johnny G, Smitty, and Booker—thank you for making me laugh and helping me pay the rent. Game nights with you are the highlight of my week.

Deborah Price, your insights into the psychology of money have been invaluable. Thank you for pioneering the path in behavioral money coaching.

To my former clients, your trust was the foundation of my career as a financial advisor. Serving you was an honor I took seriously every single day—at least after I stopped drinking.

To my fellow travelers on the road to recovery, your support has been my lifeline. Keep holding the line.

And finally, to all who shared your stories and expertise, enriching this project beyond measure—my deepest gratitude.

Here's to all of you who contributed to this journey, knowingly or unknowingly. This book is as much yours as it is mine.

www.ingramcontent.com/pod-product-compliance
Lightning Source LLC
Chambersburg PA
CBHW071646210326
41597CB00017B/2127